Guillaume Berville, Edward Walford

The story of the Chevailer Bayard

Guillaume Berville, Edward Walford

The story of the Chevailer Bayard

ISBN/EAN: 9783742840295

Manufactured in Europe, USA, Canada, Australia, Japa

Cover: Foto ©Andreas Hilbeck / pixelio.de

Manufactured and distributed by brebook publishing software (www.brebook.com)

Guillaume Berville, Edward Walford

The story of the Chevailer Bayard

"*SPOTLESS AND FEARLESS.*"

THE STORY OF
THE CHEVALIER BAYARD,

FROM THE FRENCH OF THE LOYAL
SERVANT, M. DE BERVILLE,
AND OTHERS.

WITH NOTES AND INTRODUCTION BY
THE EDITOR.

Fifth Edition.

LONDON:
SAMPSON LOW, MARSTON, LOW, AND SEARLE,
CROWN BUILDINGS, 188, FLEET STREET.
1875.

CHISWICK PRESS:—PRINTED BY WHITTINGHAM AND WILKINS,
TOOKS COURT, CHANCERY LANE.

CONTENTS.

	Page
INTRODUCTORY ESSAY	ix—xx

Chapter I.

Parentage and birth of Bayard. Death of Aymond Terrail. The Bishop of Grenoble. Bayard's first tournament. Bellabre and the Abbot. Generosity of Bayard . . 1

Chapter II.

Bayard follows Charles VIII. into Italy. Bayard distinguishes himself. Death of the king 19

Chapter III.

Louis XII. succeeds to the throne. Bayard gives a tournament. Italian towns submit to Ludovic Sforza. Bayard is taken prisoner. Generosity of Sforza 23

Chapter IV.

Ludovic is attacked and defeated in Novarra. Ludovic is taken prisoner. His death. Other Italian towns are conquered. Generosity of Bayard. Naples is conquered. Treaty with Ferdinand of Arragon. Adventures of Bayard. Don Alonzo prisoner. His escape and re-capture. Bayard challenges Don Alonzo. Death of the Spaniard 30

Chapter V.

Bayard's thanksgiving. A truce is proclaimed. Bayard skirmishes with Spaniards, is victorious. Dispute with Tardieu. Bayard's usual generosity 41

CONTENTS.

CHAPTER VI.

Engagement at the Garilliano. Bayard is taken prisoner and recaptured. Julius II. hostile to France. Illness of Bayard. Bayard takes a mountain fort. Paul de Novi beheaded. Further victories in Italy. Padua surprised, and retaken by the Venetians. Count of Pétigliano occupies Padua. The emperor with Chabannes and Bayard take Montselles and encamp before Padua. Hot fighting at the barriers of Vicenza. Enormous booty. Treason in the camp. Skirmishes. Malvezze is attacked and routed. He escapes. Bayard is congratulated. 44

CHAPTER VII.

Skirmish with Scanderbeg. Guignes Geoffrey takes a prisoner. Bravery of the young soldier. Bayard takes the Castle of Bassano. Valuable booty. Dispute between victor and vanquished. Chabannes is perplexed. Bayard solves the difficulty. Germans refuse to go to the breach 65

CHAPTER VIII.

Departure of the Emperor. Return of the armies to Vicenza. Separation. Bayard at Verona. His exploits. Bayard meets Manfroni. Foraging party surprised. Bayard's horse is killed. Bayard victorious 76

CHAPTER IX.

Treachery of a spy. Captain Sucker does good service. Bayard defeats Manfroni. Bayard well received in Italy. French reinforcement. Lignago is taken. Death of Cardinal d'Amboise. Shocking cruelty. Return to Montselles. Meeting with Croates. Lord Mercure and his cousin. Re-taking of Montselles . . 84

CHAPTER X.

Julius II. declares war against Ferrara. Another treacherous spy. Total defeat of the French. Death of Malherbe. Gritti's stratagem fails 97

CHAPTER XI.

Julius II. and La Mirandola. Bayard and others prepare to aid the Countess. Bayard lays a plan 104

CHAPTER XII.

The Pope saved by a snowstorm. Severe frost. The Countess capitulates. La Mirandola taken. Julius contemplates the reduction of Ferrara. He determines to take La Bastia 108

CHAPTER XIII.

Bayard the Counsellor. His advice is taken. La Bastia approached. Defeat of the Pope 113

CHAPTER XIV.

Anne Sforza. Death of the Lord of Montoison. Duke of Urbino opposes the siege of Ferrara. Julius plans to take the town by surprise. Horrible treachery of the Pope. Surprise of Bayard. Disagreement of the Duke and Bayard 119

CHAPTER XV.

Julius returns to Rome. Marshal Trivulce retakes La Mirandola. Glory of Bayard. Bayard accompanies Chabannes. A duel. Venetians besiege Verona. Bayard avenges the Baron of Conti's death. Army stops at Carpi. A marvellous astrologer. Fortune-telling. Strange predictions. Duke of Nemours goes to Ferrara. The siege of Bologna is raised 127

CHAPTER XVI.

Brescia. Juvenile quarrel. Brescia taken. The castle holds out. After much fighting Brescia is retaken. Bayard wounded. Conveyed to a neighbouring house. Generous and friendly conduct to its inmates. The Duke de Nemours visits Bayard daily . . 138

CHAPTER XVII.

Bayard is convalescent. The surgeon takes leave of him. Affecting interviews between Bayard and his host's family. Bayard's generosity. Bayard receives presents, and takes his leave . . . 153

CHAPTER XVIII.

Bayard goes to Bologna. Captain Jacob. Opinions are divided. Ravenna is cannonaded. The Baron of Bearn and Bayard go out to skirmish. They retreat in good order. Battle is ordered for Easter Sunday 158

CHAPTER XIX.

A bridge is built. Conversation between Bayard and Don Pedro de Paes. The battle of Ravenna commences. Captain Jacob dies. The Duke of Nemours dies. Total defeat of the Spaniards . . 168

CHAPTER XX.

Letter of the Knight Bayard to Laurent Alleman, his uncle, on the battle of Ravenna 181

CONTENTS.

Chapter XXI.

Obsequies of the Duke of Nemours. The Pope's orders disregarded. The Cardinal de Médicis escapes. Engagement at Pavia. Bayard wounded. Bayard visits Grenoble. He fêtes the nobility. A gallant adventure. Bayard's noble mindedness. Bayard follows the army to Pampeluna. The lansquenets refuse to fight. A successful adventure. An amusing lansquenet. The siege of Pampeluna is raised 165

Chapter XXII.

Bayard's hospitality. Julius II. dies. French retreat from Italy with great loss. Henry VIII. nearly taken prisoner. Bayard is taken prisoner, and takes a prisoner. Their dispute is settled. Louis marries Mary, sister to Henry VIII. Louis dies, and is succeeded by Francis I. Colonna is taken prisoner 198

Chapter XXIII.

Bayard narrowly escapes death. The Swiss are entirely defeated, and return to their country. The king is knighted by Bayard. Ferdinand of Arragon is knighted 218

Chapter XXIV.

A dauphin is born. Bayard saves the town of Mésières . . 223

Chapter XXV.

Bayard returns to France, where he exercises his generous qualities 235

Chapter XXVI.

Lodi is taken. Bayard is made to occupy a dangerous post. Bayard is mortally wounded 238

Chapter XXVII.

Generosity of the Marquis of Pescara. Bayard dies. Character of Bayard 245

Additional Notes 253

Epitaph of Bayard 255

INTRODUCTION.

THE name of Bayard[1] is very familiar to all of us English, who love bravery and a career of adventure; but the story of the life of the Spotless and Fearless Knight is very little known. It is now two centuries and a-half since Etienne Pasquier wrote that he endeavoured "to refresh and restore the memory of a good knight almost buried beneath the ingratitude of years." And his later French biographer, M. Henry D'Audigier, writing in 1862, quotes these words, which we cannot do better than adopt. For such a memory is worth restoring, not because the man was a brave soul, but because he was generous, just, merciful, a despiser of mere riches,

---

[1] Bayart and not Bayard. We write the name as our hero signed it himself. The President Salvaing de Bossiero, in the 17th century, criticised the common orthography, and said: "*Bayartius sic enim vocandus, non ut vulgò, Bayardus.*" So M. D'Audigier. We have been, however, constrained to use the spelling now so thoroughly accepted in France, Spain (whence perpahs *Bayardos* the first deflection), Germany, and England, that the true name looks strange and pedantic; and thus Shakspere, perhaps though the more correct, looks somewhat like an offence to those who prefer the chivalric and heroic *Shake-spear.*

a model of manly virtues, cheerful as the day, witty, modest, and full of that kind of "pluck," to use a common but expressive word, which always rose to its greatest height in any danger, rose with the danger, and faced it to the last; moreover, because he carried out fairly and truly Wordsworth's character of the happy warrior, who in sudden danger was not cast down, but—

> "Happy as a lover; and attired
> With sudden brightness as a man inspired."

And because he will recall to modern ears, says M. D'Audigier, "those old and too little remembered words, honour, duty, justice, loyalty, liberality, gallantry and gaiety" (the gladness of good sense, and a pure conscience, that fine humour which inspires strong and healthy souls), "all noble and charming things, once signified by a single word *Chivalry*, of which one *Chevalier*[2] Bayard was the very personification, the best that is found in our annals."

"Three qualities," says the Loyal Servant, "marked him for a perfect soldier; he was a greyhound for attack, a wildboar in defence, and a wolf in retreat. In short," concludes this excellent writer, his friend and secretary,

---

[2] Knighthood and knight would be the exact translation of *chevalrie* and *chevalier*, but of course in our tongue the strict import of the words has been lost, since the government makes knights of successful timber merchants, plotting lawyers, grocers, who deliver an address, and mere citizens, who by chance fill the office of mayor when royalty passes by, or its guest honours the city. As it would be impossible for any one to understand M. D'Audigier's graceful antithetical figure by the meaning affixed to the words *knight* and *knighthood*, I have retained the French form.

"it would take a good orator his life to recount all his virtues; I, who am unskilled in learning, cannot pretend to it." And yet, though he puts it thus, he paints with such skill, that it is a pity that his book should die. In his pages we see and hear the good knight, and behold him always joyous and merry, a true gentleman of the grand old school, remounting a poor knight, by exchanging a Spanish charger, worth 300 crowns, for a sorry nag worth six, and persuading the gentleman that the latter was *just the nag to suit his purpose*. He was but a poor flatterer, and always spoke the truth, even to the greatest princes. He looked with contempt on this world's wealth, and was at his death no richer than at his birth. "In war none excelled him; in conduct he was a Fabius Maximus; in enterprize, a Coriolanus; in courage and magnanimity, a second Hector."

As the grandfather and great-grandfather of Bayard fell fighting against the English, and the good knight himself crossed swords with us, and was a prisoner to our king, it seems to me a worthy thing to put his life before a nation that always loved the qualities which distinguished him; moreover the book is full of interest, and although it ends tragically—if a glorious death be tragic—is yet, as its originator calls it, a right joyous, pleasant, and refreshing history, full of most interesting pictures, described by an eye-witness, who speaks not like an uncertain chronicler, but as one who had seen what he described. This gentleman (possibly Jacques Jeoffre of Millieu, see p. 244), who has not let posterity know his name, but who calls himself "The Loyal Servant," put forth his book in 1527, three years after the hero's death, and from that the following title-page is transcribed:—

La tres joyeuse plaisante
recreative hystoire, compose par le loyal serviteur des faiz
gestes triomphes et prouesses du bon chevalier sans paour
et sans reprouche le gentil Seigneur de Bayart dont
humaines louenges sont repandues par toute
la chrestiente De plusieurs autres bons vaillans
et vertueux capitaines qui ont este de son
temps. Ensemble ses guerres batail-
les rencontres et assaulz qui de
son vibant sont survenes
tant en France Espai-
gne que Italie.

Paris, 1527.

This work is the basis of every life that we have of Bayard, and it is so well written and amusing that others have done well to do little else but copy it. In 1616, M. Théodore de Godefroy,[3] published a quarto volume, with a portrait of Bayard, probably about as unlike him as a portrait[4] well can be, and being little else but the story of the Loyal Servant reprinted in more modern French, with the addition of 100 pages of annotations, chiefly without interest.

---

[3] Histoire du Chevalier Bayard, Lieutenant-Général pour Roy au Gouvernement de Dauphiné, &c. &c., by Théodore Godefroy. Paris, 1616.
[4] It represents the chevalier as a hard-featured man, with a Saracen's-head look, in armour, with a hand leaning on his helmet. The armour has the merit of being somewhat like the armour of the age in which he lived, though the casque has an impracticable visor. Our own portrait has a Roman helmet, but is the received likeness of Bayard adopted from his bust set over his tomb in the Church of the Minims, founded by his uncle the Bishop of Grenoble.

In 1789, at Grenoble, a place dear to Bayard, M. Gagnon fils, avocat au parlement, made a grand Historic Eulogium on Bayard, in which he repeats many of the gestes and feats of the knight, and this *éloge* was honourably mentioned. In 1834, M. Cimber, of the Bibliothèque Royale of Paris, published, in his collection of curious archives in the history of France, four curious works (he says six, but two are suppressed), which relate to Bayard, some contain his moral sayings, the fourth compares him with "three Gentiles, three Jews, and three Christians;" the sixth contains orations, lamentations, and epitaphs. The first of these books was composed by Messire Symphorien Champier, doctor and knight, and has been used for the sake of annotations, though it contains little worth studying; from the last we here translate the following proverbs and moral answers of Bayard, and transcribe a song, worthy to be remembered on account of its quaint sadness.

"One day a noble knight asked Bayard what goods and chattels a gentleman should leave to his children?

"Answered the knight, 'The father should leave that which fears no rain, tempest, or the force of man, or the weakness of human justice, that is, wisdom and virtue, like indeed unto him who would plant a garden, and put therein good seed and sound trees.'

"Said another to him: 'What difference is there between a wise man and a fool?'"

"'The same,' said he, 'that there is between a sick man and his doctor.'

"Another said to him with a sneer, 'Well, Bayard, certes I can behold goodly lands, and worldly riches, but I never can clap my eyes on that prudence and wisdom that you have so much praised.'

"*Respondet* knight Bayard, 'Certes, I wonder not at

all that you see earthly goods, for you have eyes of earth, earthy, but you have not the eyes of heaven, to behold prudence, and to catch sight of wisdom.'

"One day Bayard heard two young pages swearing by the name of God, and he punished them very severely.

"'Knight Bayard,' said a gentleman, 'you punish these boys for a very little thing.'

"'Little thing!' cried the knight. 'A bad habit contracted in youth is no *little* thing, but a great thing indeed.'

"The good knight said many other moral proverbs, but they have quite slipped my memory."

Thus far the chronicler, and considering how good those are that he has given us, we must be sorry that they have done so.[5]

In 1699, Aimac, a barrister, (avocat), published at Lyons a life of Bayard, at which we have glanced, and which is well characterized by M. Petitot,[6] as forming a little volume in 12mo., and being written with extreme meanness (d'une grande médiocrité). In 1702, a new history of Bayard appeared in Paris, in 12mo., under the name of the Prior de Louval, the true author being the Canon of Avalon. "His book," says M. Petitot, "is merely that of the Loyal Servant painfully translated into the modern tongue."

In 1760, M. Guyard de Berville published a "Histoire du Bayard," which ran through many editions. "This

---

[5] M. Cimber adds that "Bayard once told a lord that he should only surround himself with worthy people, and it appears that it is to him that we owe this proverb, 'Like master, like man.'" *Tel maître, tel valet.* Valet did not then signify the menial thing it does now, but a follower in the field of battle.

[6] Collection complète des Mémoires relatifs à l'Histoire de France, depuis le règne de Phillippe-Auguste, jusqu'au commencement du dix-septième siècle, &c., par M. Petitot. Paris, 1827.

work," says Petitot, "is weakly written, and is only valuable on this account, that its author has neglected nothing which can make us better acquainted with our hero." The truth is that M. de Berville has taken from Champier, Godefroy, and others, all that he could, has given the dates of the episodes, connected the story by relating the political history which led to the various battles, and has made the memoirs of the Loyal Servant thoroughly connected and historical. As to its weakness, that should disappear in a vigorous translation did it exist, but it does not. In all that relates to our hero, De Berville copies the Loyal Servant so closely, that Southey's vigorous English reads as a mere translation of De Berville : hence his book has been used as the basis of the present volume.

In 1825, Robert Southey translated, or caused to be translated, the life of Bayard from the book of the Loyal Servant. It was published by Murray in two volumes, but is carelessly done. Every now and then the translator misses the sense of the author, and some words, such as *grande-buffe*, he utterly mistakes; nevertheless there is fine and vigorous English about it, as there is in all Southey's work, and we have availed ourselves of the book and its annotations, whereby we have found that our book has been made more complete and interesting. In 1848, Edward Cockburn Kindersley published a condensed translation in English of the Loyal Servant's work, to the notes of which, some of them furnished by Mr. Albert Way, we confess our obligations. And in 1862, M. Henry D'Audigier[7] pub-

---

[7] Histoire de PIERRE TERRAIL, seigneur de Bayart, dit Le Chevalier sans peur, et sans reproche, par Henry D'Audigier. Paris, 1862.

lished a volume, which is a kind of romance, written in the subjective style which Lord Macaulay made so popular in England, but which every scholar knows to be so false. Thus, when a late pictorial writer describes our Saviour as having his face suffused by a modest blush when he stooped down to write that awful and marvellous sentence in the dust: "Let him who is without sin amongst you cast the first stone;" relative to the woman taken in adultery, everyone feels that the assertion is impudent and untrue. The judge does not blush for the woman; a blush assumes a perturbation of feeling utterly foreign to the nature of the Incarnate. So when Mr. H. Dixon, in his Holy Land, describes the Saviour and his apostles, as if he had been at their elbows noting down the little idylls, as he queerly calls the miraculous works of the anointed Christ, we feel that the realism is impertinent and false, and that it utterly misses its aim; so also this writer's exquisitely *outré* phrase, with which he commences one of his chapters, shocks us plain men: "On the whip hand, as you enter Jerusalem, you observe," &c. This might have been written by an Arab, did an Arab carry a whip, but not by a writer who was barely a fortnight in the city with which he is so marvellously familiar.

In a like manner we think that M. Henry D'Audigier has failed through want of taste in his story of Bayard. He has "reported" speeches that were never made, described certain days as fine, full of sunshine, or black with rain, to suit his purpose, and has produced a novel, not a history. It is, no doubt, very vivid, but a little thought entirely overthrows the scaffolding, and makes great holes in the canvas, painted to look like stone. But M. D'Audigier has a noble comprehension of our hero, and to his book and its notes we are indebted for some interesting facts in this introduction. To various other histories and works[8] we are also indebted.

To those who think of kings and royal personages as beings able to use their brains, and to recognize and reward talent,—a light in which, as boys with many romantic illusions, many of us loyally regard them,—one will wonder that Bayard was so little regarded and recompensed by his monarch. "I have lost a great captain, whose name made *my armies* to be honoured and feared, and truly he merited better employment and higher charges than ever I gave him." That is what Francis I. of France said of him; and afterwards, as he well had cause, he was heard to murmur: "Ah! Captain Bayard, *how much I do miss you.*"

A strange confession for such a king. But what does it amount to, says M. D'Audigier. Francis thought of Bayard, no doubt; but why? because his interests suffered, not his heart. Kings make use of their Bayards, but they love only their Bonnivets.

Henry IV, as it was fitting, passing by Grenoble in 1601, remembered Bayard, and asked was there no monument to him. He said he would have liked to have raised a tomb to so pure, so beautiful a fame; but words did not ripen into deeds. In 1619 the government of the province voted a thousand livres for a statue; but it was only a vote—they could not spare them. What, could not the descendants of those hundred orphan girls —noblewomen and gentlewomen—whom the good

---

[8] Especially to "Archives curieuses de l'Histoire de France, depuis Louis XI. jusqu'à Louis XVII; ou Collection des pièces rares et intéressantes, celles que chroniques mémoires, &c., par M. L. Cimber et autres personnes employées à la Bibliothèque Royale." Paris, 1834.

knight had dowered with his property, " sans en faire bruit," without making any fuss about it, spare a livre or so? asks a writer. No, it was not to be so. About 1650, a private gentleman, neither relation nor connection of the knight, named Scipio de Polloud, raised a white marble bust to his memory in the church of the Minims, on a tomb surmounted by a Latin epitaph, of which we have given a copy; and at last, in June, 1823, three hundred years too late, a statue was raised at the Place of St. André, Grenoble, to the memory of Bayard. The artist had to draw from imagination, for history supplies but a vague guide for him to work from; but what boots it?

Bayard's daughter, Jeanne, married, one year after her father's death, François de Bocsozel, Seigneur de Chastelart, and her descendants are represented in 1823 by Madame d'Attenas, née Bocsozel, who was invited to the inauguration of the too tardily raised statue. George, the only brother of the good knight who married, died without heirs male, and the last holders of the name of Terrail, issue of a cousin of our hero, died out, in the latter half of the seventeenth century; so that the name Bayard alone survives: that name (I remember with pleasure) was, by common consent, applied to my revered friend Sir James Outram, one as widely appreciated and as generally neglected as the good knight—who himself died with the plain " Sir" before his name, the Bayard of India.

The castle in which Bayard was born is only about ten minutes' walk from Pondcharra. From it you have an admirable view of the valley of Grésivaudan, the convent of the Grande-Chartreuse, and the mountains of Beauges. Entering a dilapidated gateway, one beholds two ruinous structures. One of these, which was a chapel, is now a stable. The other serves for the dwelling of the steward of the property. "The principal tower had three stories, of which the first only remains. They still show the chamber of Bayard, and that in which Helene of Allemans first saw the light. The stables, the cellar, and the refectory and kitchen are well preserved; all the rest is completely destroyed. The Duc of Berry, just before his assassination, had ordered one of his friends to buy the château, intending to restore it and to make it a princely residence, but the poniard of Louvel put an end to that dream."[9]

But if kings did not appreciate the good knight, we shall see in this history that his enemies, his friends, and his companions did, and it is worth while to rescue from oblivion this sad song of his companions.

Lamentation et complaincte par manière de chanson de la mort du bon Bayard faicte par les avanturiers au retour de Lombardie.

> Aydez-moi tous à plaindre,
> Pouvres advanturiers,
> Sans poinct vous vouloir faindre,
> Ung si noble pilier!
> C'estoist le singulier
> Sur tous les gensd'armes;
> Car dedans un milier
> Une tel n'avoit en armes.
>
> Le jour de Sainct Estroppe,
> Bayard, noble seigneur,
> Voyant les ennemis en troppe,
> Il monstra sa valeur.
> C'estoit par faveur
> De la faulce canaille,
> Dont luy vint ce malheur
> Mauldicte soit la bataille!

---

[9] Itinéraire descriptif et historique du Dauphiné.

> Plourez, Plourez, gendarmes
>   A cheval et à pied;
> Car jamais d'homme d'armes
>   Ne vous en veinst pis.
> Il a tenu bon pied
>   Sans faire au Roy tort
> Dont à luy fut le pis
>   Car gaigné a la mort.
>
> Le vaillant chevalier
>   Il pensoit nuyct et jour,
> Comme pourrait bailler
>   Au genx du Roy secours.
> Adonc il prit le cours
>   Contre ses ennemys,
> Dont ses jours en sont cours,
>   Vous voyez mes amys.
>
> Ha pouvre Dauphiné,
>   Tu peulx bien dire hélas!
> Avant qu'il soit finé
>   Tu en seras bien las.
> Tu as perdu ton solas,
>   Et encore de rechief
> Tu peulx bien dire hélas!
>   Il te coustera cher.

And with this sad echo of the old free-lance companions of the good knight, the editor and translator take leave of their readers, wishing them a full enjoyment and noble appreciation of these joyous and pleasant feats and gestes of the good knight, and repeating the farewell words of the Loyal Servant in excuse for any shortcomings: "But as for what I have said herein, I do beg all readers of this history to take it kindly and in goodwill, for I have done the best that I could, though not, indeed, all that was due to the praise of so perfect and virtuous a person as the good knight without fear and without reproach, the gentle Lord of Bayard, whose soul may God in His grace grant to rest with Him in Paradise. Amen."

SPOTLESS AND FEARLESS.

CHAPTER I.

BAYARD, whose goodness and valour, intrepidity and prudence, coolness and presence of mind, patriotism and piety, gained him one of the noblest reputations ever acquired by a soldier, and the all-envied title, "Le chevalier sans peur et sans reproche," was born in 1476, while Louis XI. was on the throne of France. The château Bayard, in Dauphiny, was his birthplace, and when Guillaume d'Avençon, Archbishop of Embrun, came into possession of the estate, and found that the castle wanted repairs, he gave orders that the room which Bayard had occupied should be kept untouched, out of respect to the memory of so great a man.

Historians who have written his life have told us little of the earliest years of the boy who distinguished himself so much as a man. Doubtless he passed them as other children do, in receiving instruction, and joining others of his age in the amusements then general.

When still a child, hardly thirteen, his father, who felt that his end was approaching, sent for his four children, their mother being present, to ask them what professions they chose. The eldest declared his wish to live with his parents as long as they lived, and to enjoy his inheritance peaceably afterwards. Bayard, the second, spoke after his brother, and, with a spirit astonishing in one so young, said that, holding so glorious and illustrious a name—a name unsullied and untarnished by numerous ancestors who had borne it, and who had glorified it by incomparable feats of arms—he begged leave to try and imitate them. That was his wish, and he hoped, by the help of God, never to take one sparkle from the glory of those of his house whose high deeds he had often heard with such thrilling pleasure. The father was moved to tears by the zeal and earnestness of the boy. "My son," said he, "you are already in face and figure like your grandfather, who was one of the most accomplished gentlemen of his time. I am rejoiced at your resolution, and I will do all I can to forward your wishes, by placing you in the house of some prince where you will learn all noble and manly exercises fitting for a knight."

Aymond Terrail lost no time, but the next day sent for his brother-in-law, the Bishop of Grenoble, to consult with him as to what should be done. The good bishop came with many more knights to a banquet which Aymond had prepared, and at which the young Bayard served with a grace and modesty that drew praise from all present. After the banquet, the old man told them how he had questioned his sons, and of the answer of Pierre, the second, dwelling upon the delight he felt at his choice, and begging them to advise him what house of prince or noble to send the boy to. Each gave his word of advice. One said, make him page to the king; another, in the house of Bourbon; but the good bishop said, "You know well how friendly the Duke of Savoy is to our house; he is now at Chambéry; to-morrow we will set out, and I will present my nephew to him for a page; be at no expense, for I myself will equip and mount him."

All applauded; and the father, leading the young Bayard to the bishop, with tears in his eyes, said, "I give him to you, and pray God that wherever you place him he may do you honour."

Then the bishop sent to Grenoble for dresses for the child, and all was ready by the next day, so that Bayard, well equipped and mounted, presented himself before the company with as good a grace as if he had been in the presence of the Duke of Savoy. The horse, accustomed to a heavy weight and feeling the spurs, gave two or three alarming bounds, but the young chevalier kept a firm seat and managed his horse with the skill of a man of thirty. All were astonished at the courage of a boy just free from the schoolroom, and mounted for the first time. His father asked him if he felt no fear. Bayard, with perfect coolness, answered, that he hoped by God's help to manage his horse among the enemies of the prince he was going to serve.

His father took an affectionate leave of him, and his mother, a pious, good woman, mixed her tears and her kisses with wholesome advice, which sunk deeply into the heart of the boy, and had who can tell what effect upon the future life of her darling. She begged him, above all, to serve God first, to pray to him night and morning, to be kind and charitable to all, to beware of flatterers and never become one himself, to avoid envy, hatred, and lying, as vices unworthy of a Christian, and to comfort widows and orphans. Bayard replied lovingly and modestly; and, provided with a purse and a little trunk containing his linen, he and his uncle took their way to Chambéry, where they arrived the same day, Bayard happier than he had ever been in his life before.

The next day the prelate waited upon the duke,[1] who was rejoiced at his visit, esteeming him one of the most virtuous and pious prelates of his time. The duke kept a brilliant court, and had always been a faithful ally of France. He received the uncle and nephew with all signs of friendship, and pressed them to remain and dine with him. They did so, and Bayard waited upon his uncle at table with so much grace that the duke was impressed with his manners, and asked the bishop who the child was.

"Sir," said the old man, "he is my nephew, whom I have brought to present to you, if his services will be of use to you."

"I accept him at once," replied the duke; "I should indeed be difficult to please if I refused such a present."

The young knight delighted at this, and, having been previously instructed by his uncle what to do, did not wait for dinner, but immediately went out and dressed himself to appear advantageously before the duke. His horse was beautifully caparisoned, and as he approached the palace, where the duke was seated at a window, he managed the mettlesome steed as well as if he had passed all his life on horseback.

"My lord bishop," said the duke, "is that your nephew yonder, who rides so charmingly?"

"Yes, my lord," replied the bishop, "it is my nephew; he comes of a good family, and one which has produced brave gentlemen and valiant knights. His father, overcome with old age and covered with wounds, has not been able to bring his son himself, so he has commissioned me to do it for him."

---

[1] This was Charles I. son of Amédée IX. and Yolande of France, daughter of Charles VII. He had succeeded his brother, Philibert I.

"I am only too happy to receive such a present," said the duke, "and if he walk in the steps of his ancestors I shall have abundant reason to thank you for your gift."

So Bayard was installed a member of the duke's household, where he applied himself so heartily to all knightly exercises that he carried away the palm from all his comrades; he surpassed them in the dance, on the lute, in passages of arms, and, more especially, in horse exercise. He was so graceful, and manly, and obliging to all, that the duke and duchess looked upon him as their own son.

Six months after, the Duke of Savoy set out for Lyons, where Charles VIII. had been for a year with his court, and amused himself amongst other things with tourneys, feasts, and balls given to the ladies of the town, and even did them the honour to admit them to his table. The king, hearing of the duke's arrival, sent the Count de Ligny[2] with a number of gentlemen and a detachment of archers to meet him. They met them at about two leagues from Lyons. The prince welcomed heartily the Count de Ligny and the Lord d'Avesnes,[3] and all the other lords and gentlemen, whence they returned together talking merrily on the way. The count perceived the young Bayard in the procession, and was so charmed with his horsemanship that he could not help

---

[2] Louis of Luxembourg, son of Louis Count of Saint-Pol, Constable of France, who was beheaded at Paris, the 19th of December, 1475, for the crime of felony.

[3] Gabriel d'Albret, Lord of Avesnes, brother of John d'Albret, King of Navarre. John was the father of Jane d'Albret, married to Antoine de Bourbon Vendôme, by whom she became the mother of Henry IV. in 1553.

complimenting the duke upon it. The duke told him that he was a nephew of the Bishop of Grenoble, and still very young. He called to the boy and ordered him to gallop, crying out, "Spur, Bayard, spur!" Asking no questions, young Bayard did as he was ordered, and at the end of the run he brought the horse back curveting and bounding, but perfectly manageable. The count again praised the youth, and said how glad the king would be to have him in his service. The next day, at the table the conversation turned upon the chase and horses, from those the transition was easy to tournaments, war, and gallantry. The Count de Ligny told the king of the page of fourteen who was so brave a horseman, and said if his Majesty wished to see him he could do so as he went to vespers at the abbey of Ainay. Bayard was soon informed of this, when he hastened to the Duke of Savoy's groom and begged him to make his horse look better than ever before. The groom, who loved the boy, promised. Bayard went immediately to dress himself, so that he might appear at his best, and was ready when his friend the groom brought his horse. This faithful servitor, who foresaw that Bayard was about to change masters, said to him, "My dear Bayard, whatever satisfaction I may feel at your advancement, I can but be grieved to lose you; I understand that you are going to pass into the service of the King of France; you cannot wish for anything more advantageous, nor for a better occasion to make a name and a fortune."

The hour for parting having arrived, they mounted on horseback, Bayard's horse being groomed fit for the king himself. They reached the meadows of Ainay, where the king and his suite arrived by water, a short time after, and the king had scarcely landed when he perceived the groom and the knight on horseback.

"Page, my friend," cried he, "give the spur!" The other pages repeated, "Spur, spur!" Which he did with as much skill and grace as if he had had thirty years' experience. And from the word *piquez*, spur, Bayard got his surname of Piquet, by which he was known for a long time after. The king was charmed with the young page, as the duke had been before him, and committed him to the care of the Count de Ligny, who was delighted with the acquisition. He placed him among his pages, and at the end of three years, when Bayard was seventeen, the count made him a man-at-arms in his company, and gentleman of his house, with three hundred livres a year.

The Duke of Savoy remained at Lyons several days; and during his stay a nobleman named Claude de Vaudray, of the province of Burgundy, asked the king's permission to give a tournament for the young nobility. This tourney was to consist of horse-racing, and of combats on foot and on horseback, with lances and battle-axes. The king, who loved all these symbols of war, easily granted permission, and the Lord of Vaudray[4] attached his coat-of-arms to a post, so that any gentleman who wished to enter into the lists could touch it and afterwards give his name to the king-at-arms of the tourney. Bayard, who had been a man-at-arms for some days, passed with one of his comrades before the post, and remained silent before it, tempted to add his name to the list. "Alas!" said he, "if I only knew how

---

[4] Maréchal de Gié. His arms were per pale, gules, and argent. This house, a very illustrious one in the county of Burgundy, had for its device, "J'ai valu, vaux, et vaudrai,"— I have been worth, I am worth, I shall be worth; in allusion to three territories belonging to it, Vaux, Valu, and Vaudray.

to obtain what is necessary to fit me for the combat, I would willingly touch these escutcheons."

His comrade, named Bellabre,[5] a gentleman like himself belonging to the household of the Count de Ligny, surprised at his sudden fit of musing, asked him the cause.

"Ah, my friend," replied Bayard, "my hand is longing to touch that shield, but when I have done so, who is to provide me with horses and necessary accoutrements?"

Bellabre, a little older and more worldly-wise than he, said to him, "Why trouble yourself about that, my friend; haven't you an uncle in the neighbourhood, the Abbot of Ainay?[6] If you like, we will go together and pay him a visit, and if he refuse to give you money, why, I'll seize crosier and mitre, and anything else I can lay my hands upon."

"No, no, my friend," said Bayard, "let us respect the church and her ministers."

"I hope," replied Bellabre, "that we shall not have to resort to violence; when your uncle knows what you require, and that the king is your friend, he will be generous enough, depend upon it."

Bayard, encouraged by his friend, hesitated no longer, but immediately advanced and touched the escutcheons.

The king-at-arms, Mountjoy, who was placed there

---

[5] Pierre de Pocquières, Lord of Bellabre, of Limousin. He was all his life Bayard's friend, and followed him in most of his campaigns.

[6] The Abbot of Ainay was not Bayard's uncle; he was three or four degrees removed. His name was Theodore Terrail. He held his abbey forty-eight years, and died there in 1505. . His tomb may still be seen in the centre of the nave.

to receive the names of the combatants, was astonished at the boldness of the young man, and said to him, "Why, Piquet, you are only a child yet, and do you mean to put yourself against the Lord of Vaudray, who is one of the boldest knights in Christendom?"

"Mountjoy," replied Bayard, "if I have touched that shield, believe me it is neither pride nor vainglory that has prompted me. I wish to learn the glorious profession of arms from those who are capable of giving me lessons, and, God helping me, I hope to acquit myself to the satisfaction of the ladies."

The king-at-arms smiled; he could not help admiring the resolution and wisdom of the youngster of seventeen. Soon all the town knew that Bayard was to take part in the approaching tourney. The report reached the ears of the Count de Ligny, who was overjoyed, and went to tell the good news to the king. The king was equally charmed, and said to the count, "My cousin, I have presented you with a pupil who will gain you honour."

"I hope, sire," replied the count, "that he will come well out of this affair; but he is very young to measure himself against this Lord of Vaudray."

But the most difficult part of the preparations was still to be gone through; money was necessary to a splendid appearance. "I don't know," said Bayard to Bellabre, "how to approach the Abbot of Ainay if you do not introduce the subject. I am sure that if my uncle the Bishop of Grenoble were at home he would give me anything I wanted, but unfortunately he is at the Abbey of Saint Saturnin, at Toulouse; even if I wrote to him there is no time to wait for an answer."

"Be easy," replied Bellabre, "we will visit the abbot to-morrow, and I promise you to get the money from him."

The next day the two friends crossed the Saône to Ainay. They had hardly disembarked when the first man they saw was the abbot himself, reading, in a meadow. They approached him respectfully; but the abbot, who had already heard what had passed, and who guessed what this visit meant, did not receive them very cordially, and asked Bayard how he came to be so absurd as to touch the shield of M. Claude of Vaudray.

"Three days ago," said the old man, "you were a page, you are hardly eighteen years old; you deserve a good whipping for showing so much vanity."

"My dear uncle," modestly replied the knight, "I protest that vanity has nothing whatever to do with this. I have no other design than to show myself worthy of the honour of belonging to you and a house in which valour has always been hereditary; so I beg you, sir, to help me with money. You know that I have neither relation nor friend near but yourself to whom I can apply."

"My faith," replied the abbot, severely enough, "you must beg elsewhere; the wealth of the church has been given for prayers to God, and not to supply money for tourneys."

Then Bellabre spoke. "Sir, without the merit and valour of your ancestors you would not be Abbot of Ainay. You are under an obligation to them for the glory they have acquired, and to their name which you bear. You owe them gratitude, and how can you pay the debt better than by doing good to your nephew? Up to this time he has done you credit; he is a favourite of the king and of the count our master, who has already made him a man-at-arms in his company. The king, even, knows he is to fight; and you ought to be charmed with his spirit of emulation, and do all in your power to contribute to his advancement. Perhaps it will cost you two hundred crowns to equip him, and in return he will gain you honour to the amount of ten thousand."

The abbot replied, and Bellabre once more answered him so well that the uncle finally consented to assist his nephew. He accompanied the young men to his house, and, taking a purse from a cabinet, he took a hundred crowns, and gave them to Bellabre, saying, "Young gentleman, take care of this money, and buy two horses for this brave soldier; his beard is still too young for me to trust him with it. I will send word to Laurencin to furnish him with all necessary garments."

"I thank you for him," said Bellabre, "and for my own part, reckon on my gratitude; we will not forget to talk about your kindness."

The abbot then wrote to the merchant to furnish the young man with the stuffs necessary for him to appear honourably at the tourney. The two friends, armed with the letter, immediately went to the merchant to whom it was addressed, and each one bought three similar suits, for Bayard wished his friend to appear there with his money, for they were such good friends that one had nothing that he did not share with the other. Only horses were wanting now. An occasion soon presented itself. A Piedmontese gentleman, who had only been at Lyons a few days, had fallen and broken his leg. He had two horses, which he determined to sell instead of feeding them and getting no work in return. Bellabre, who heard of this circumstance, spoke of it to his friend and took him to the sick gentleman's apartments, with whom the bargain was easily concluded. They tried the horses first, after which the price was fixed at a hundred and ten crowns for the two. The money was paid, and two crowns given to the grooms who led the animals to the stables of their new masters.

There were now only three days before the tournament, which Bayard and his friend employed in becoming acquainted with the tempers of their new steeds.

The tournament commenced on Monday, the 20th July, 1494. The Lord of Vaudray distinguished himself and did marvels; also Jacques Galyot de Genouillac, Lord of Aster, Seneschal of Armagnac, who was afterwards Grand Equerry of France, and Grand Master of the Artillery; Germain de Bonneval, Louis de Hédouville, Lord of Sandricourt; the Lord of Châtillon, of the house of Coligny; the Lord of Bourdillon, and a number of others; most of them honoured with the king's friendship. It had been ordered that each one, after fighting, should go round the lists with his face uncovered, that the spectators might judge whether he had fought well or ill.

The knight Bayard, then in his eighteenth year, still weak and delicate in appearance, took his place in the lists and struck his first blow, which was considered too bold for one so young. Whether for this reason the Lord of Vaudray favoured him, or whether his skill and strength conquered, certain it is that the majority of votes were for him, and the ladies especially, in their patois, praised him loudly, and said that he had done better than all the others.

The king was charmed as well as his people, and said to the count at supper, "By the faith of my body, cousin de Ligny, Piquet has given us to-day a foretaste of what he will be as a man. He is the best present I ever made you in my life."

"Sire," replied the count, "the honour will redound to your Majesty, and to that thought he owes the glory that his achievements have thrown over him."

About a year after the tournament the Count de Ligny took Bayard aside, told him that, in addition to his place of page-in-waiting, he had put him in his company of artillery. He then sent the overjoyed young man away to join his comrades, saying, " You will find among them some of the most valiant men in France, daily practising warlike exercises, and you cannot do better than remain with them till war demands your services."

Bayard was overjoyed; he thanked the count with his whole heart, for, as he said, "the greatest favour he had ever received." He begged permission to start the next day, and, having obtained it, went with his master to take leave of the king. The king was just leaving table.

" Sire," said the count, " your Piquet has come to bid your Majesty farewell before joining his companions in Picardy."

Bayard fell on one knee before the king with a modest yet self-possessed air. The prince looked at him graciously and said, " Piquet, my friend, may God continue in you what I have seen begun; may you grow up a brave man. You are going into a country where beautiful ladies abound, do all you can to gain their good graces; and now, my friend, good-bye!"

Bayard thanked the king with respect, and then took an affectionate leave of the princes and of his comrades. The king, calling one of the valets-de-chambre, ordered him to give the knight three hundred crowns, and added to the present one of his finest horses. Bayard, out of gratitude, gave thirty crowns to the valet-de-chambre, and ten to the groom who brought the horse. This first act of generosity increased the esteem of those who heard of it. As Bayard was to set off early the next morning the count bade him adieu overnight and counselled him with the affection of a father, recommending him to keep in the paths of religion, honour, and virtue. Bayard kissed his hand, and moistened it with his tears, and then took his final leave, followed by the gentlemen and officers of the household, who embraced him tenderly and assured him of their sorrow at his departure. At the same moment the count's tailor brought him two rich suits of clothes, by his master's orders, and a groom arrived with the finest horse from the count's stables completely harnessed. The knight, surprised at so many presents added to those he had already received, gave the tailor twenty crowns, and the groom ten, begging them to thank their master for him, as he did not feel equal to the task.

At daybreak he sent off his six best horses, after them his carriages, and he himself followed with his remaining horses. Bellabre, his friend and companion, could not accompany him to his destination as he was awaiting the arrival of two horses from Spain; but he went several miles with him, and promised to rejoin him soon.

Bayard journeyed by easy stages to keep his horses fresh; and when he was about six miles from Aire in Picardy, he sent an attendant forward to prepare his lodging. As soon as his comrades heard of his approach, they came out to meet him on horseback to the number of a hundred and twenty, thinking they could not show too much honour to a man so well thought of by their king and their captain. They met at about a mile and a half from the town, and having greeted each other with expressions of esteem, they conducted him in triumph to their quarters. Many ladies were at their windows, for they had heard so much of the virtues, the wisdom, and the high-mindedness of Bayard, that they were impatient to see him.

Part of the company remained and took supper with

the new comer, and his success at the tournament was the principal subject of conversation at the meal.

"Friends and companions," said Bayard, with his usual modesty, "I have not had time to deserve the praises that you are lavishing upon me; but, by God's help, and following in your steps, I hope one day to be worth the name of soldier."

One of the company named Tardieu, a merry good-humoured fellow, and a thorough lover of pleasure, addressed himself in his jovial manner to Bayard: "Comrade," said he, "I hope you haven't come to the garrison without a well-filled purse, because the ladies in these parts are very fond of tournaments, and they have not had the pleasure of seeing one for a long time. Give them one eight or ten days hence."

"If you will undertake to obtain the commander's permission, and send me the herald," said Bayard, "it shall be as you wish, my friend; it will give me even more pleasure than you."

Tardieu felt certain that the captain, Louis d'Ars,[7] would not withhold his consent. However, it was time for the party to separate, and they did so, promising to meet again early the next day.

Tardieu was the first to arrive; he entered saying, "Comrade, here is your herald, now you can settle everything."

Although the knight, fatigued with a long march, had required rest, he sat up the greater part of the night writing the proclamation, which was ready when Tardieu entered. It was to this import, that—"Pierre Bayard, a gentleman of Dauphiny, in the service of the high and

---

[7] One of the most illustrious captains of his time. He was a native of Dauphiny, a relation and neighbour of Bayard.

mighty lord, Count de Ligny, lately initiated into the mysteries of war, publishes a tournament for the 20th of July, outside and close to the walls of the town of Aire, to all comers, to fight with lances without lists, and on horseback; the prize for the conqueror to be a gold bracelet enamelled with his arms, of the weight of thirty crowns—that the next day will be fought a combat with lances on foot, and after the lances are broken an assault with battle-axes, the prize for which will be a diamond of the value of forty crowns." Tardieu highly approved of the proclamation, and vowed that Launcelot, Tristram, and Gawain were not to be compared to Bayard. They gave it to the herald, and bade him proclaim it in that town, and in all the garrisons in the province. For in those days there were a great many companies of brave knights, who all heard of the approaching tournament. All those who wished to take part in it hastened to Aire; and, notwithstanding the shortness of the notice, they arrived to the number of forty or fifty.

In the interval the valiant captain Louis d'Ars arrived, glad to be there in time for the tournament. As soon as Bayard knew he had come, he went to pay his respects to him, and was received in the most flattering manner. To heighten his joy his good friend Bellabre arrived the day after his commander, and had a flattering reception from every one. Then there were nothing but fêtes and balls, where Bayard showed so much grace, and prudence, and generosity, that the ladies of the town, and those of the province, could do nothing but praise him; they unanimously gave him the preference, curiously enough, without making him vain, or his companions jealous.

At last the day arrived, Louis d'Ars, and the Lord of St. Quentin, captain of the Scotch guards, were appointed umpires. The number of combatants was forty-six, whom the judges divided into two parties of twenty-three against twenty-three. This done, and the combatants being ready to enter the lists, the herald sounded his trumpet and published distinctly the order of the tournament. Then the knight appeared first on the scene, and Aymond de Salvaing, lord of Boisseau,[8] his cousin, was the first opponent who presented himself; this man was surnamed "the Tartar," as Bayard was called " Piquet," according to the custom of the times. They ran one against another so furiously that Boisseau broke his lance short in two, and Bayard awaited him on guard and shivered his lance in pieces. Immediately two trumpets sounded to announce this brave assault. Bayard finally conquered. After them came Bellabre, and a Scotch captain named David of Fougas. The Tartar, the captain David, the Bastard of Chimay, Tardieu,[9] Bayard, and his friend Bellabre were amongst the most successful combatants.

At the end of the day Bayard, who had prepared a magnificent supper, invited those who had taken part in the tournament, and a number of ladies. The repast was followed by dances and other amusements until one o'clock in the morning, when everyone retired. The next day, according to the order of the tournament, they began again; and after attending mass, as it was Sunday, they dined with the lord of St. Quentin. The meal was not of long duration, for as the clocks struck two the

---

[8] Aymond de Salvaing was the grandson of Catherine Serrail, the aunt of Bayard.

[9] John of Tardieu, a gentleman of Rouergue. He was a man-at-arms in the company of the Count of Ligny before Bayard, in connection with whom he will be met with several times in this history.

trumpet called the combatants to the barrier. The umpires, the lords, and ladies being placed, Bayard entered first as on the previous day; his adversary was Harmotin de Saker, a gentleman of Hainault; Bayard soon forced him on his knees, and then the judges called out, "enough, enough!"

After them Bellabre entered the lists against Arnaulton de Pierreforade, Tardieu fought against David of Fougas, and the whole company declared that they had never seen so many skilful brave men assembled at one tournament. After the supper, to which they repaired at the close of the tournament, the question was to be decided as to who should receive the prizes. The judges took the opinions of the company—first the ladies were appealed to, and begged to say frankly and without partiality who they thought had distinguished himself the most. All voices, gentlemen's and ladies', were raised in favour of Bayard; and St. Quentin, after the trumpet had sounded for silence, handed the jewels to the young knight to give them to whomsoever he thought most deserving after himself. Amidst the praises of the company he awarded one to his friend Bellabre, and the other to the Scotch captain, David of Fougas.

During the two years that elapsed from Bayard's arrival in Picardy, till the departure of the king for the kingdom of Naples, he frequently gave tournaments, in the greater number of which he came off victorious. He gained universal esteem and friendship, and the ladies were never tired of praising his prudence and numerous virtues.

CHAPTER II.

N 1494, Charles VIII. determined to claim, by force of arms, the rights he had upon the kingdom of Naples. He entered Italy at the head of a large army, traversed the country without interruption, and on the thirty-first of December, with the whole of his troops, entered Rome by torchlight, and with the lance in rest. He there did several acts of sovereignty; appointed some criminals to be executed and pardoned others, while Pope Alexander VI, famous for his crimes, not being able to oppose the king, retired to the Castle of Saint Angelo. The king forced him from his retreat and compelled him to crown him Emperor of Constantinople and King of Naples; afterwards he set out to make the kingdom submit, leaving for viceroy Gilbert, Count of Montpensier, a prince of the blood royal.

The Count of Ligny, who followed the king in this expedition, took Bayard with him, not only because he liked him, but because he wished to give him an opportunity to distinguish himself.

The king, after a glorious campaign, left a large part of his army to guard his newly-acquired kingdom, and went back to France with less than 10,000 men.

On his road, near Fornova,[1] he was unexpectedly attacked by an army of 60,000 men, composed of the pope's troops, of Venetians, and of the soldiers of the Duke of Milan and other Italian princes. Their design was to surprise, defeat, and carry the king away. A prize of 100,000 ducats was promised to the man who brought him to the camp, dead or alive. Six ducats were moreover offered for every Frenchman's head; but heaven ordered it otherwise.

Charles, although compelled to fight with such a handful of troops, gained a complete victory;[2] 10,000 of his enemies were left upon the field, and he only lost 700 of his men; the slaughter would doubtless have been greater, but the sudden rising of a small river hindered the king from profiting by his success.[3] The enemy lost almost all their generals, especially the Venetians; many nobles of the house of Mantua perished, and the marquis himself owed his life to his spurs and the swiftness of his horse. Bayard, who was in the king's army, in De Ligny's company, distinguished himself more than any one, and had two horses killed under him. He took an ensign from fifty men-at-arms and presented

---

[1] A town in the Duchy of Parma, three leagues south of that city.

[2] Amongst the gentlemen who fought at Fornova were a number of lords of Dauphiny with their companies, all composed of the nobility of the province; but as it would take too much space to enumerate them all, we will only mention the Serrails, Allemans, Sassenages, Clermonts and others who acquitted themselves with much valour.

[3] The approach of night forced the combatants to separate, the king being resolved to finish on the morrow what he had so well begun; but, in the interval, a stream which divided the two camps rose to the height of seven feet and overflowed, saving, no doubt, the remains of the combined army.

it to the king, who, already informed of the courageous ardour that he had shown in this action, granted him 500 crowns. It was in this battle that Jacques de Cize-de-Chambarau fought, a gentleman of Dauphiny, whose whole family, both male and female, were of gigantic height. He was then one of the king's guards, and his family became extinct in Henry IV.'s reign.

Charles, after his glorious exploits at Fornova, advanced to Verceil, where he found a considerable body of Swiss ready to help him; he raised the siege of Novarra, where Ludovic Sforza, calling himself Duke of Milan, kept besieged, Louis Duke of Orleans, afterwards Louis XII. The nobility of Dauphiny, who had done such wonders in the last battle, signalized themselves before Novarra, but they lost three of their number, Peter of Sassenage, Charles Alleman (Bayard's uncle), and Barachim Alleman, his cousin-german, Lord of Rochechinard, Knight of Malta, and Grand Prior of Provence.

The king, after these expeditions, returned to France and went to Lyons, where his queen, Anne, and his sister, the Duchess of Bourbon,[4] had arrived on their way to meet him. Arrived, with all his Court, at Paris, he visited the tombs of his ancestors at St. Denis, as if he had foreseen that, although only twenty-six, it would not be long before he joined them. The next two years he passed in visiting his kingdom, showing his subjects a shining example both of religion and morality. Finally, he went to Amboise, where he heard of the general revolt of the kingdom of Naples, the triumphal entry of Frederic, the death of the Count of Montpensier, and the forced return of his troops. He

---

[4] Anne of France, wife of Peter of Bourbon, lord of Beaujeu.

resolved to return in person for the reduction of this kingdom, and set out in September, 1497, for Lyons, but he only got as far as Tours; he returned to Amboise to pass the winter there, and died suddenly in the month of April following, watching a game of tennis, aged only twenty-eight years. His four children, by Anne of Brittany, died before him.

CHAPTER III.

[1498.]

CHARLES VIII. having died without children, his brother-in-law, Louis, the Duke of Orleans,[1] succeeded him. He had married Charles's sister Jane, but was speedily divorced from her. The pope having proclaimed the marriage null, the lady retired to the Duchy of Berry, which the king gave her, and died seven years after in the odour of sanctity. Louis, having settled the divorce, married the queen dowager, Anne of Bretagne.[2]

While the new king was attending to the internal affairs of the country, Bayard was visiting his friends in Savoy, in the house of the duke where he had been r

---

[1] He was then thirty-six years old, and was the son of Charles, Duke of Orleans, whose father, Louis I, brother of Charles VI, had married Valentine of Milan, from whom he derived his right to the duchy. The mother of Louis XII. was Maria of Cleves.

[2] " Whether it (the divorce) were ill or well done, God knows," says the Loyal Servant. Anne's marriage contract with Charles VIII. contained this singular clause, that in case she became a widow she could only marry the king's successor; this was done to render more sure the union of her duchy of Bretagne with the crown of France.

page. Charles I, his old master, whose memory was still dear to him, was dead, and his widow, Blanche Paléologue, the heiress of Mont-Serrat (daughter of William VI. and Elizabeth Sforza) was at Carignan in Piedmont, which had been given to her as dowry. She was a virtuous and generous princess, and had always entertained as much friendship for Bayard as the late duke, her husband. Her Court was as brilliant as any in Europe, and strangers were received there with royal magnificence. The wife of the Lord of Fluxas, who was the superintendent of the duchess's house, was one of her maids when Bayard first entered the house as page to the duke. She was beautiful, witty, virtuous, and belonged to a good family. Bayard was endowed with the same advantages, and a friendship commenced between the young people, which soon ripened into love. And, if fate had been propitious, they would doubtless have been united in marriage; but the duke's journey to Lyons and the entrance of Bayard into the king's service separated them so entirely that from that time until his present visit they had only communicated by letter. He found her advantageously married to the rich and powerful Lord of Fluxas. When she saw the knight she received him with every sign of friendship. She had heard of his exploits and congratulated him upon them, and they talked over their boy and girl passion for each other. She finally asked Bayard to give a tournament, to which he immediately consented, and said it should be in a few days. Bayard kissed the lady's hand, and asked her for one of her sleeves. The lady gave it him and he put it into the sleeve of his doublet, intending it for the victor's prize. The herald proclaimed the tournament, and brought the names of fifteen gentlemen who promised to be there. The day having arrived, Bayard and the Lord of Ronastre first entered the lists; Bayard was victorious. The tournament lasted all day, and at the close of it the Lord of Fluxas, by the duchess's commands, invited all the gentlemen to supper with her, and while at table the judges awarded the prize to Bayard. Bayard blushed, and refused it. He said that the lady who provided the sleeve[3] should give the prize. She said she would keep the sleeve herself for the sake of the victor, and as he refused to receive the prize she gave a ruby pendant to the Lord Mondragon, who, next to Bayard, had been the most successful combatant The prize was then delivered and the customary ball began ; the gaieties were continued four or five days, after which each gentleman returned to his garrison. The duchess was overjoyed to see her quondam page so generally esteemed and respected, and so beloved that no one was jealous of him.

A short time after, Ludovic Sforza, who had retired to Germany, had raised a considerable army there of Swiss and Burgundians, and a fine body of German cavalry. With these troops he entered Lombardy, and on the 3rd of January he surprised the town of Milan, and drove the French from it. Following the example of the capital, several other towns submitted to Sforza, and the king, hearing of the fresh revolt, sent a powerful army under the orders of the Count of Ligny and De Trivulce, to reduce the rebels to subjection.

Bayard had remained in Italy, by permission of the Count of Ligny. He believed that Ludovic would

---

[3] M. de Berville has "bracelet" here, while the "right joyous history" reads sleeve, which is more in keeping with the manners of the time; it was probably the heraldic *manche* worn still as a charge in coats of arms.

soon return and cause more trouble than on his first
campaign, in which Bayard had not taken part. His
ardent wish to excel in his profession kept him continually on the watch for occasions to distinguish himself and serve his prince. He was in garrison then,
twenty miles from Milan, where he passed the time with
his comrades in military exercises. One day he was
informed that there were three hundred horse in Binasco
that might be easily defeated. He spoke of it to his
companions who were only too glad to join him in
undertaking it; so they set off early the next morning
to the number of about fifty officers to try the adventure. Jean Bernardin Cazache, the captain on the
other side, who commanded in Binasco, was brave and
alert. He learnt from his spies that a French party
was coming to attack them. As soon as the two troops
perceived each other they commenced the fight, the war-
cry on the one side being " France! France!" and on
the other, "Moor! Moor!" The charge was brisk, and
a great many were thrown from their horses, and others
with great difficulty retained their seats. But Bayard
seemed like a furious lion. He made the heads and arms
fly with unparalleled dexterity and rapidity. Seeing that,
after an hour's fighting, the victory was not yet decided
in his favour, he cried out, "What, my companions!
shall we let this handful of men keep us here all day?
Courage, my friends, let us redouble our blows, and
overturn them." These words reanimated his men;
each one felt a new ardour, and again crying, "France!
France!" they fell upon their enemies with such impetuosity that they drove them from the place. The
French followed them four or five miles towards Milan;
but the Lombardians, finding themselves near the
town, turned their horses and thus saved themselves,

the French still chasing them. When the French were near the walls, one of the principal and the most experienced, seeing the danger, cried, "Turn, men-at-arms, turn!" Every one obeyed except Bayard, who was too excited to hear. He pursued the fugitives with so much ardour that he entered Milan with them and chased them as far as the king's palace. The white crosses that he wore soon caused him to be recognized as a Frenchman, and the people cried out, "Take him! Take him!" He was surrounded in a moment, and taken prisoner by Cazache, who took him and disarmed him. He was surprised to see one only twenty-four years old giving signs of such extraordinary valour.

Ludovic, hearing the noise and the uproar, asked the cause: they told him of the defeat of the captain Cazache, and that a young Frenchman had pursued the fugitives even to the palace. He was curious to see him, and commanded him to be brought. Cazache was told to present himself with his prisoner before Ludovic; he was afraid that Ludovic would be in a fury, and cause him to be assassinated.

"My good gentleman," said Ludovic to the knight, "come here, and tell me what has brought you to this town."

Bayard, who was never astonished at anything, freely replied, "I had no idea that I was alone; I thought my companions were behind me; but they are wiser than I, and more used to the ways of war, or they would undoubtedly have been made prisoners as well as myself. In the meantime, in my disgrace, I thank heaven that I have fallen into such good hands as yours."

Ludovic then asked him the number of the French army.

"Sir," replied Bayard, "I do not think that there are more than 1400 or 1500 men-at-arms, and from 16,000 to 18,000 foot soldiers, but they are all picked men, and resolved to make the duchy of Milan submit at once and for ever to the king their master; and for you, sir, I assure you, you will be safer in Germany than here, for your men cannot possibly resist us."

The duke appeared amused at the certainty with which Bayard spoke, but it gave him something to think of. Nevertheless, he hid his fears under a show of bravery, and gave the young knight to understand that he wished for nothing more ardently than a meeting between his troops and those of the king of France.

Bayard replied that nothing would give him greater pleasure also, provided he were not in prison.

"Set your mind at rest," said the prince, "it is my intention to set you free. Ask anything you like of me, and I will grant it you."

The knight had not expected such generosity. He knelt on one knee to thank him. "Sir," said he, "the greatest favour I can ask of you is to restore my arms and my horse, and allow me a guide to the garrison twenty miles distant; and, believe me, I shall always be ready to serve you, if I can do so in honour to my king and to my country."

The duke ordered Cazache to restore his arms and horse, which that noble officer was only too ready to do. The horse having arrived, Bayard vaulted into the saddle with his usual grace and agility, and again thanking the duke for his generosity, departed with the guide.

Ludovic was far from rejoiced at what had happened. Although he admired the courage and sang-froid of Bayard, he naturally thought that if all the men of the

French army were like him, he himself would not be likely to prove victorious.

On Bayard's arrival at the camp, he presented himself to his general, the Count of Ligny, who was much astonished to see him. "What, Piquet!" said he, "are you out of prison? Have you paid your ransom? I was about to send a herald to pay it, and bring you back."

"Sir," replied Bayard, "I thank you sincerely, as I ought. Ludovic has spared you the trouble, and proved himself a rival in generosity even to yourself—he has allowed me to return without ransom." He then related to him and a crowd of officers who were present the whole of the adventure from first to last; and, in reply to the Lord Jean Jacques, who asked him if he thought Ludovic would risk battle, he replied that Ludovic had not given him to understand as much as that, but that he was a man not easily astonished, and one for whom they must be always ready. "As for me," he continued, "I can only praise him; and all I know is, that the greater part of his men are in Novarra, and that to do anything he must either join them or order them to come to him."

CHAPTER IV

WE have previously said that Ludovic had entered into Milan, but that the citadel still remained in the possession of the French. When he saw the king's army so near him, he was afraid of being hemmed in between it and the citadel, so he went away secretly in the night to Novarra, taking almost all his followers, and leaving the rest in Milan, with his brother, the cardinal. Just at this critical juncture, La Tremouille joined the Count of Ligny and Trivulce, and they resolved to attack Ludovic in Novarra. Ludovic's troops were strong in number, but composed of Burgundians, Swiss, Lansquenets, and German cavalry. They were, in consequence of their variety, difficult to govern. Thus, in a few days, the town fell into the hands of the French generals. This happened the Friday before Palm Sunday.

It was reported that the prince was not in the town, and that he had escaped to Germany. Whether he was betrayed or not is not certain; it was ordered that the foot-soldiers should pass under the halberd, and Ludovic, pressing amongst these in the dress of a common soldier, was recognized and made prisoner, set free on parole,[1]

---

[1] Ludovic Sforza was carried prisoner into France, at first to Pierre-Encise, at Lyons; afterwards to Lis-St.-George's, at Berry; and, finally, to the castle of Loches in Touraine, where he died in 1510.

and the rest of his army were allowed to march away. Ludovic Sforza, with bag and baggage, was conveyed to France, and, after being a prisoner at Lyons, in Berri, and in Touraine, successively, died in 1510. It is very certain that, before the engagement, the Swiss had mutinied, either because their pay was irregular or at the instigation of Antoine de Bessai,[2] Grand Bailiff of Dijon, who was in great repute amongst them. It has also been hazarded that they would not fight against their numerous countrymen in the king's army. Such a determination would speedily decide the loss or gain of a battle. Whatever it was, Ludovic deserved a happier fate if he had fought for a better cause. He was brave, generous, and beneficent; but his good qualities failed to insure him against the caprices of fortune.

When his brother, the cardinal, learnt that he was a prisoner, he quickly sent his two sons to the Emperor of Germany, and was himself proceeding to Boulogne with an escort of 500 or 600 horse, but he was stopped on the road by Severin de Gonzagua, captain of the Venetians, who sent him to the French, and took care of the booty, money, and baggage, the value of which they estimated at two hundred ducats.

The rebels at Milan did not know the fate of their princes whom they had submitted to the king, and they fully expected their town to be plundered, but they found the king and his generals more magnanimous than they merited, for they entirely pardoned them.

---

[2] Antoine de Bessai, baron of Senchâtel, and of an old and illustrious house in the county of Burgundy. He was held in high esteem in the Swiss Cantons, and it was he who was commissioned by the king to raise a body of 15,000 Swiss for the conquest of Milan.

Louis, wishing to reward his officers for the services they had rendered him at Milan, had given them, as fiefs, several places in the duchy; amongst others, he gave Tortona and Voghiera to the Count of Ligny, besides several smaller places. They had all followed the example of the capital, and submitted themselves to Ludovic. The count resolved to punish them for their treachery. He took with him the famous captain Louis d'Ars. Bayard, and several other officers. When his subjects knew his intentions, and that he had already reached Alexandria, resolved, as he said, to destroy them by fire and sword (although this was a mere threat), they were extremely alarmed, fearing a destruction which they knew they deserved. They selected twenty of their best men, and sent them to their new master to sue for mercy. This deputation met him at a few miles from Voghiera, but he appeared not to notice it, and continued his way to the town. The suppliants, exceedingly frightened, followed him, and implored Louis d'Ars to intercede for them. This, with his usual generosity, the gallant captain promised to do, and told them to visit the count the next day. In the interval, he informed the count of the visit he might expect, and begged him to pardon the miscreants.

The next day, after the count's dinner, fifty of the principal citizens appeared, and presented themselves on their knees and bareheaded before him. A very eloquent man among them begged for mercy in a soul-stirring speech; but the count appeared inflexible, and treated with the utmost disdain the large quantity of silver they had brought him as a peace-offering. The poor fellows were in great distress, and thought that certain death must be their fate, when Louis d'Ars stepped forward, and, with his hat in his hand and one knee on the ground, pleaded for them, for the sake of God and His Son Jesus Christ.

The count was moved almost to tears. "Go," he said, "I pardon you for the sake of the Captain of Ars, whose services deserve even a better return than that. As to your silver, I cannot accept it." Then, turning to Bayard, "Piquet, take all this, it will adorn your table."

"I thank you," replied Bayard; "God forbid that the wealth of traitors and unfaithful subjects should be used by me; they would do me harm." So saying, he took the plate, piece by piece, and distributed it amongst those present, not keeping one for himself. Then he left the room, and the deputation followed him. When he was gone, all the company began to speak of the generosity of Bayard. They all agreed that he would be one day one of the most perfect of men. The next day, to reward him for his generosity, the count presented him with a magnificent velvet dress, a valuable horse, and a purse containing three hundred crowns, which he immediately shared with his comrades.

A few days after, the count returned to Milan, where the Cardinal d'Amboise had just arrived as lieutenant-general for the king in Lombardy, and thence returned to France.

The treachery of the Neapolitans, and the loss of that kingdom, would certainly have been revenged by Charles VIII. had he lived. Louis XII, his successor, began his reign with the conquest of Milan, so that his intended vengeance upon Naples was postponed.[3] Fer-

---

[3] It was during this campaign of 1503 that Bayard, offended by Hyacinth Simonetta, a man belonging to a noble Milanese house, of merit and valour, but insolently arrogant, challenged

dinand, the son of Alphonse, in whose favour the rebellion was raised, was dead, and his uncle, Frederic, had succeeded him.

During the life of Charles, the Count of Ligny had married Eleanor de Baux, princess of Altemore. The house of Baux was ancient and illustrious; it was a Provençal family, which had removed to Naples. When duty called the count away, the lady felt it so deeply that she died of grief. By her death and the king's munificence, De Ligny possessed many lands and houses in the kingdom, particularly in La Pouille, such as Venoye, Canose, Monervine, Berjeilles, and others. Louis having resolved to make Naples submit to him, the Count of Ligny had hoped to command the king's army there, but his plan was twice frustrated, and it is believed that vexation for the disappointment occasioned his death, which happened, a short time after, on the 31st of December, 1503.

Bérault Stuart,[4] Lord d'Aubigny, was appointed by the king to command his army. He was a wise, brave officer, then captain of the Scotch Guard. The army was compact and numerous, both in infantry and cavalry. The Count of Ligny's company was under the orders of

---

him to a duel and killed him. We only find this in Alcyat, a Milanese jurisconsul, who, without relating either the cause or the circumstances, says, "I have seen knights who, too much affecting goodness and grace under arms, have let victory escape them. Such was Hyacinth Simonetta, a Milanese gentleman, who fought against Bayard, a French captain, during the first inroads of the French to Italy. It was a manifest presage of the overthrow of Sforza, which happened soon after."

[4] The president Henaut (Abrégé Chron.) and the Abbé Lavocat (Dict. Hist.) call him Robert Stuart, but his real name was Bérault. He died in 1548.

Louis d'Ars. Bayard took leave of his old master with great friendship expressed on both sides, and much regret.

D'Aubigny marched straight into Naples, and with such speed, that Frederic, taken by surprise, and little loved by his subjects, was unable to defend himself, and had no other resource but to make the best conditions possible. He made his treaty with the French general, by whom he was told that he would be taken into France with his wife and his children,[5] and that he would have for appanage the enjoyment of the duchy of Anjou for life. He was received by the king with the honour due to his dignity, and the treaty was strictly observed while he lived; but after his death, in 1504, his widow was so neglected that she fell into a sad state of indigence and misery.

Naples conquered, the companies were garrisoned in the kingdom. The Count of Ligny's company went to the lands that belonged to that nobleman, and Louis d'Ars made Bayard governor of a quantity of the possessions of De Ligny. He acquitted himself to the satisfaction of everybody.

About the same time another treaty was made with Ferdinand, King of Arragon, husband of Isabella of Castille, father of Jane the Fool, and grandfather of Charles V. Ferdinand had claims upon a part of the kingdom of Naples, which was given to him by the king. By this treaty peace was made between the two princes and with the Emperor Maximilian, and pub-

---

[5] Frederic married one of his daughters to La Tremouille. From that circumstance that house claimed rights to the crown of Naples, and the eldest sons bore the title of Princes of Tarento.

lished at Lyons the same year. The mediator was the Archduke Philip, son-in-law of Ferdinand; he also drew up the treaty, which was soon violated, and while Louis was resting securely upon the faith of Ferdinand, the latter sent a powerful army to Ferdinand Gonzalva, called the *great captain*, his lieutenant in those parts which had been ceded to him. These troops entered into the kingdom of Naples by the connivance of Pope Alexander VI, took the capital, and drove the French from almost all parts of the kingdom. D'Aubigny opposed them as long as possible; but, at last, forced to yield to numbers, he retired to La Pouille, where he remained a long time—till the year 1504, when, after having engaged in a great number of battles, gained some and lost others, the French were obliged to leave the country.

But let us return to our hero during the sojourn of the French in La Pouille. Being in garrison at Monervine, he was tired of doing nothing, and proposed to his comrades that they should go out and search for stray parties of Spaniards whom they might overcome. The proposition was received with joy, and they set out at daybreak resolved not to return without having seen and encountered the enemy. On the same day, the Spanish captain, Don Alonzo de Soto Mayor, had proposed to go out and meet the French; and Bayard and Alonzo were both equally pleased at the thought of a contest when the numbers were so well matched. The numbers were about equal. When the good knight recognized the Spaniards by their red crosses, he turned round in his saddle, and said to his troop, " Now, my friends, here is just what we came to look for; here is some honour to be gained. Let us do our duty. If you don't see me do mine, hold me all my life as a poltroon."

" Charge! " shouted the company; " don't let us give

them the honour of attacking us." Then, lowering their visors and putting their horses to the gallop, they fell upon the Spanish troop, crying, "France! France!" On their side, the Spaniards returned the cheer with "Spain! Spain! St. Jago!" and, with lance in rest, received them vigorously. At the first shock a great many were dismounted on both sides, and their companions had a great deal of trouble to remount. The affair lasted for about half an hour, each striving for victory. The second attack was on the flank. At last, Bayard so inspirited his men by word and example that the Spaniards were defeated. They left seven on the field and as many prisoners; the rest took to flight, their commander Soto Mayor with them. Bayard pursued him and called upon him to stop if he did not wish to be slain from the rear; not wishing to die an ignominious death, he turned. They fought, and the Spaniard yielded to the Frenchman, after displaying courage only second to that of Bayard himself. The French did not lose a single man in this skirmish, although five or six were wounded. Bayard behaved nobly to his prisoner, treating him with all the honour due to so distinguished a soldier, and leaving him free, on receiving his word of honour that he would not go beyond the castle walls. Wearying of his captivity, although he was as free as prisoner could possibly be, Don Alonzo planned his escape. He bribed an Albanian named Théode to provide two horses, by means of which they could both reach the nearest garrison of the Spaniards. Théode, who had a great affection for money (of which he was promised a large sum by Alonzo), consented to aid his escape, and they set off, Alonzo intending to send Bayard his ransom, the price of which had been fixed at 1000 ducats. Bayard, soon after their departure, came round to have his usual talk with his prisoner, but he was nowhere to be found. Bayard's rage and indignation at the departure of the Spaniard and the Albanian were indescribable. He ordered eleven of his faithful servants to ride towards Andres, and overtake the fugitives. They had scarcely gone two miles when they perceived the two not far distant. Alonzo was on foot attending his horse's saddle-girths. Before he could remount he was fallen upon by Bayard's men and brought back to Monervine. Bayard, as may be imagined, severely reproached him, and treated his petty excuse of ennui with contempt. He was then confined to one of the towers, but in all other respects treated as before. At the end of fifteen days a herald and one of his valets arrived with his ransom, and he was set at liberty. He remained just long enough to take leave of Bayard and the other officers, and to see the whole of his ransom money distributed amongst the soldiers.

Upon Don Alonzo's arrival at Andres he was questioned as to the character of Bayard. He praised the character of the man, but complained of the way in which he had been treated as a prisoner, saying he would resent such conduct to his dying day. His hearers were divided in their opinions, some sympathised with their countryman, others thought Bayard in the right, while others again consoled him with the remark that "prisons were never beautiful places."

It came to Bayard's ears that Don Alonzo complained of his treatment while he was his prisoner; he called all his company together and asked them, as honourable men, to tell him if they had ever by word or deed treated the Spaniard in a manner to be complained of. They all answered that they had treated him as they would wish to be treated under similar circumstances. Thereupon Bayard sent for his secretary and dictated a challenge to Don Alonzo. The herald by whom he sent it brought back a reply saying that Don Alonzo would meet Bayard within fifteen days, at two miles from Andres, or in any other place which seemed good to him. Bayard, who was far from well, accepted all the terms of the challenge, and having obtained permission to fight from the Lord of La Pallisse, lieutenant of the Duke de Nemours, he chose his old friend Bellabre for a second.

When the day arrived Bayard was first upon the field, mounted and dressed in white. The Spaniard had not yet arrived, and the herald was despatched to hasten his coming. Bayard had previously allowed him the choice of the manner of fighting; hearing that he was on horseback, Alonzo sent to say that he chose to fight on foot, thinking that Bayard, who was very ill, would be obliged to refuse to fight in consequence. But he had mistaken the character of the man. Bayard was certainly surprised, but he quickly recovered himself and sent back the herald to hasten his adversary, who presently arrived accompanied by the Marquis of Licite, Don Diego Quignonès, Don Pedro de Valdès, Don Francisco d'Altemez and numerous others. Chabannes, D'Oroze, D'Humbercourt, Foutrailles, Baron of Bearn, and many more had come with Bayard to the field. The combat was of long duration. Bayard, notwithstanding his weakness, fought with his usual skill and bravery. After some time, during which Alonzo managed to keep even with his adversary, Bayard thrust his long sword into the Spaniard's throat, and parrying the blows which the enraged Spaniard aimed at him, he waited till the loss of blood had considerably weakened him, and then, flinging himself upon his adversary, they rolled together in the dust, Bayard giving Don Alonzo a poniard thrust between the nose and the left eye. He then called upon him to give himself up, but the Spaniard was dead. Bayard was deeply grieved that he had killed his adversary, but the deed could not now be undone, and he flung himself on his knees and thanked God for giving him the victory. He then went to the umpire, Don Diego, and asked him if he was satisfied with what he had done? "You have done too well for the honour of Spain," Don Diego replied, sorrowfully. "As the body is at my disposal," said Bayard, "I give it to you; I heartily wish I could give him back to you alive." Then, amidst great cries and much lamentation, the Spaniards bore the dead body away, and the French carried back the conqueror to the sound of trumpets, hautboys, and numerous other instruments.

CHAPTER V.

HEN he reached home, his first act was to proceed at once to the church, where he a second time offered up thanks to God; and afterwards gave a magnificent banquet to the officers his comrades. This combat spread the reputation of our hero over the whole kingdom.

After this event there was a truce of two months proclaimed between the French and Spanish. The Spanish were inconsolable for the loss of Soto Mayor, and vowed vengeance against the French. The officers often walked near each others' camps, and the Spaniards appeared to take pleasure in trying to insult the French.

One day thirteen Spaniards met Bayard and his good friend D'Oroze just outside the French camp at Monervine. The Spaniards saluted the two friends, and they returned their salutation.

One of the Spaniards, Don Diego de Bizagna, who had belonged to Soto Mayor's company, and was, moreover, a brave and bold knight, and could not forgive Bayard for causing his death, stepped forward, and said to Bayard, "My good French lord, the truce has only lasted eight days yet, and we are utterly tired of it; perhaps you feel the same. There are thirteen of us here; if you will form a party of thirteen against us nothing would afford myself and companions greater pleasure."

Bayard and D'Oroze looked at each other. "My Lord D'Oroze," said Bayard, "what do you think of it?"

"I know," said D'Oroze, "what answer I should make, but I would rather hear you speak."

"As you wish it," replied the knight, "I will answer." "My lord," said Bayard to the Spaniard, "my companion and I accept your proposition with much pleasure; meet us this day week at two miles distant from here. Thirteen of us will be there, and we shall see which side will conquer."

The Spaniards promised, and they returned to their sides. Bayard and his friend having related the challenge and named the rendezvous, all wished to be of the thirteen. Conditions of the fight were laid down, viz.—That if a knight lost his horse he was not to fight; that he who passed over a certain boundary should be prisoner: that the night should terminate the combat; and if there remained but one unhorsed on each side he should take back his companions with equal honour to either side.

This being agreed on, the two parties met, lance in rest, and put spurs to their horses. But the Spaniards, in the fight, basely attacked the horses instead of the men, and with such success that eleven of them were soon dead upon the field. But the Spaniards' horses refused to advance over the dead bodies, which served Bayard and his friend D'Oroze as a rampart; for they charged the Spaniards boldly and frequently, and, when attacked by many, retired behind the rampart of dead horses, so that in the end, when night set in, and they were obliged to quit the field, the two Frenchmen were unanimously proclaimed victors.

Some time after, when the truce was ended, Bayard heard by his spies that a treasurer from Naples was about to carry a large sum of money to Gonzalva, and that he would pass at a few miles from Monervine. Bayard, resolved to lay hands on the man and his treasure, set out two hours before daybreak, and went, accompanied only by twenty men, and put himself in ambush between two little hills, and he sent Tardieu, one of his men-at-arms, in another direction with twenty-five Albanians, so that if the treasurer escaped one he should be taken by the other. At seven o'clock in the morning the knight's spies heard the noise of horses, and came to announce it to him. He was so hidden by the two rocks that the treasurer and his escort passed without seeing him, and, as soon as they had gone by, Bayard and his company fell upon them, crying, "France! France! slay! slay!" The Spaniards, thinking they had a whole army at their back, fled to Barletta without looking behind them. They were pursued until the treasurer and cashier were taken, when 15,000 ducats were found in their cases. Tardieu, arriving just at this time, was dazzled by the glitter of the coin, and claimed half the prize, as he had gone on the expedition, but Bayard, who loved justice, chose to have the affair properly settled by the French general, who decided that the prize was Bayard's alone. When Tardieu saw the course matters were taking, he made a virtue of necessity and joined in the laugh against himself. Bayard, with his usual generosity, gave Tardieu half the large sum of money, and distributed the whole of the remainder amongst the soldiers. He then set the treasurer free, and allowed a herald to accompany him to Barletta, whither he wished to go.

CHAPTER VI.

OWARDS the end of the war of which we were just now speaking, the French were encamped on one side of the river Garilliano and the Spaniards on the other side. Now it must be understood that if there were brave soldiers on the one side, so there were on the other, above all, the famous Gonzalva de Cordova; but the most extraordinary of them was Pedro de Pais, who was not three feet high, and was so hump-backed and deformed that the head of his horse, when you were in front of him, hid him from your view. But, in spite of his deformity, he was one of the boldest and most enterprising of the whole army. One day he took it into his head that he would give the French an alarm, and for that purpose took with him about 120 men-at-arms, each with a foot soldier mounted behind him, armed with arquebuses, and these passed the Garilliano by a ford which they knew. When the French saw them, they thought the whole of the Spanish army had come to attack them; but Bayard, whose quarters were near the bridge, soon perceived that there were not 200 Spaniards, but that their object was to take possession of the bridge, which would have been certain ruin to the French. He immediately despatched Le

Basque to seek help, while he stood alone at their end of
the bridge, waiting for the arrival of the Spaniards; as
they approached, he fell upon them with such terrible
fury and struck such vigorous blows that he knocked
down four men-at-arms to begin with, two of whom fell
into the water and were never seen again. The Spaniards
thought they were fighting a devil and not a man; in-
censed by the loss of their countrymen, they fell upon
him with blind fury, he returning their blows with extraordinary courage; but he must undoubtedly have been
overcome by numbers if Le Basque had not arrived
with 200 men, who saved the bridge and chased
the Spaniards a good mile on the other side. They
would have gone further, but Bayard perceived a body
of 700 or 800 men coming to assist the fugitives. Thinking they had done enough for one day, he gave the
order to return, himself bringing up the rear, last in
retreat as he was always first in attack. As the troop
was marching home in good order, it was again attacked
by a detachment of the enemy. Bayard's horse was
much fatigued, and, surrounded as he was by thirty or
forty men, he knew it was useless to resist, so gave himself up to the Spaniards. His companions, who had
fought their way to the bridge, thought he was amongst
them until Pierre de Guiffrey suddenly cried out,
"Comrades, we have lost Bayard. I vow that I will
have news of him, if I go alone. Shall we leave the
man who has gained us so much glory? He is either
dead or a prisoner." There was great confusion at this
cry, and they determined to return and seek their
leader. They soon overtook the Spaniards, and called
upon them to turn and fight. They did so, and
as they had not disarmed Bayard, he joined in the
fray, and, leaving his own jaded horse, vaulted upon a

splendid charger from which Salvador Borgia had been
thrown by the lance of Le Basque. Finding himself
well-mounted, the knight fought desperately. The
Spaniards learning who it was that they had allowed
to escape, lost heart, and went off at full gallop; the
French contented themselves with watching their flight,
only too happy to retain with them their true guide of
honour, Bayard. They regained their camp without
further adventure, where they long talked of a day
made so extraordinary by curious adventures, and
especially by the exploits of the Knight Bayard.

To take up the thread of our history. We have seen
before that the French army which kept the kingdom
of Naples had been obliged to abandon it through the
numerous perfidies of Ferdinand, King of Arragon, who
violated all the treaties. Alexander VI. was dead, and
Julius II, of the house of la Rouère, occupied the holy
see, when the remnant of the French army passed through
the states of the Church. He treated the French as
well as they could possibly expect, but it was the friendship of the fox, which he made pay well in the end,
having always been a sworn enemy to the King of
France, and the whole French nation.

[1505.] Louis d'Ars and Bayard remained in Spain
after the departure of the French army, and contrived
to keep several places there in spite of the whole Spanish
army. On their return to court the king gave Bayard
a place in the household until he had a company ready
to place under his orders.

This same year [1505] was marked by three events.
The first was the death of Jeanne de France, first wife
of the king, in the town of Bourges; the second was
the severe illness of the king, who was given up by the
doctors; this circumstance possibly saved his life, for

he recovered, much to the joy of his people, by whom he was greatly beloved. The third event was the death of Frederic of Arragon, King of Naples, in the town of Tours. He held this crown from his ancestors, who had usurped it; and those who took it from Louis XII. had no more right to it than Frederic.

The next year [1506-7] was signalized by the deaths of the incomparable Isabella of Castille, wife of Ferdinand, King of Arragon, and her son-in-law, Philip-le-Beau, Archduke of Austria, who had married Jane, the eldest daughter of Isabella. Ferdinand, now a widower, married again, the same year, Germaine de Foix, niece of Louis XII. and sister of the Duke de Nemours, with whom he will often be mentioned in this history. This princess, although she had been brought up at the court of France, changed her principles when she became the wife of Ferdinand, and became a sworn enemy of her country and the royal house.

The first service that the pope rendered to the king was, by all the means in his power, to try and draw the Genoese from their allegiance. The populace, animated against the nobles, chased them from the town, and afterwards elected for doge a man named Paul de Novi. The king was informed of these proceedings, and determined to cross the mountains in person without delay, and with all the soldiers that the occasion seemed to require.

Bayard was then at Lyons, very ill with intermittent fever, and from the consequences of a wound which he had formerly received—a sword wound, which became ulcerated, but from which he fortunately recovered in time. Notwithstanding his indisposition, Bayard was one of the first to be ready for the expedition. The army was so quick in its march that they surprised the Genoese, who had no time to wait for the help which the pope and some other Italian princes were to have sent them; they nevertheless prepared for defence, and the French were astonished to find, at the top of the last mountain which it was necessary to cross to arrive at the town, a newly-constructed fort, with a good garrison and a considerable muster of artillery. Upon this the king held a council of war, and, after hearing the opinions of the rest, took the advice of Bayard, who requested permission to go with about 120 known brave comrades and see what they were doing at the fort. The king begged him to do so, and they set out, Bayard first, as always, climbing the mountain on all-fours, when they reached the top they were obliged to stop and take breath, then they marched to the bastion, having first to overcome several parties of advanced guards, who gave them some trouble, and finally fled. The French wished to pursue them, but Bayard stopped them, crying, " Do not follow them, comrades; go straight to the fort." They found 300 men there, who defended themselves pretty well for a time, but who soon took to flight, and descended the mountain precipitately, leaving many of their comrades dead on the ground. So Bayard was master of the fort, the taking of which so surprised the Genoese that their courage failed them, and they submitted at once to the clemency of the king. Louis, having entered the town, made them pay all the expenses of the war, and construct, at their expense, a citadel which commanded the town, and which he named Codifa. He had Paul de Novi and one of the nobles of the house of Justiani beheaded. He deprived the town of all its privileges, gave the people a governor in his name, to whom he obliged them to swear allegiance, and ordered that in future the coin should be marked with his arms and those of the town, after which he forgave them for all that was past.

From Gênes the king went to Savonne, where he had an interview with Ferdinand, King of Arragon, returning from Naples with his new wife, Germaine de Foix. She did not attempt to disguise her change of opinions, but treated the French nobility with insolence, not even excepting the Duke de Nemours, her brother. Her husband, on the contrary, treated them with exceeding politeness, and complimented the king upon the possession of two such distinguished soldiers as Louis d'Ars and Bayard. The French king, on his side, was not less friendly to the great captain Gonzalvo, one of the heroes of his age and nation, and of whose virtues Ferdinand was jealous. He went expressly to Naples to bring back Gonzalvo with him, fearing that, as he was such a favourite with the people, they would transform him from viceroy to king. After his return from Naples Gonzalvo passed a sorrowful life in retirement, and when he died was sumptuously buried by the king and mourned by the nation. After a few days' conferences between Louis and Ferdinand they separated, Ferdinand to continue his route to Spain, Louis to go to Milan, where Trivulce, lately become Marshal of France, gave him a magnificent entertainment, and for three days the six or seven hundred people who were gathered together enjoyed the recreation of feasts, balls, comedies, and various other kinds of amusements.

In the following year (1508) the Emperor Maximilian took up arms against the Venetians, who were allies of Louis. The king immediately sent Trivulce with a large force to assist them; but the Venetians, knowing Maximilian's rapacity for money, offered him a large sum to withdraw, which he accepted, much to the disgust of Trivulce, who was annoyed at such a cowardly proceeding.

The pride of this republic had become so unbearable that a league was entered into, called the League of Cambrai—a treaty of alliance, offensive and defensive, entered into by Louis XII, Maximilian, the Pope, and the King of Spain, to overthrow the republic of Venice. One clause of the treaty was to the effect that Louis should be in Venice forty days before any of the others. It is difficult to imagine how Louis could have signed a treaty containing such a clause, but he did so. As it turned out, he had all the success and honour of the affair, but his allies shared the profit with him.

In the month of March, 1508, the king reviewed his troops in the duchy of Milan. He appointed celebrated captains to the command of his army; to Bayard he gave the company of Captain Chatelart, who had recently died; but when he also gave him the command of 1000 infantry, Bayard begged that the number might be reduced to 500, as he feared 1000 would be more than he could manage. The king acceded to his request, and at the end of March he and all the other captains were at Milan ready for action. The king's army consisted of 30,000 men, both foot and horse. The Venetians had 32,000 soldiers under the command of Nicolas des Ursins, Count of Pétigliano.

The king, on arriving at Milan, learnt that a little town on the Adda, called Trevi, had been taken by the French and retaken by the Venetians; that the Venetians had burnt the town to punish the inhabitants for surrendering to the French, and afterwards taken prisoners the captain Fontrailles and all his men, besides several other captains who were there. The king was enraged at this, and, constructing two bridges over the

Adda, he made his cavalry pass over by one and his infantry by the other. The next day he sacked a small town called Rivolta, and two days after, on the 14th of May, the French and Venetians met at Agnadel. The Venetians did wonders, but the French gained a complete victory, and showed surprising bravery, Bayard and his men especially, who had waded through a marsh up to their waists in water. The French loss was comparatively small, but the Venetians lost 15,000 men. D'Alviano, the infantry general, was taken prisoner, and conducted to the presence of the king, who, to see if his troops were on the alert, had a false alarm made after dinner, and hearing the clanking of arms and other sounds indicative of active preparation, he asked D'Alviano what it could be.

"Your men must be fighting each other, I should imagine," was his reply; "as for our troops, I can promise you they will not soon return."

The king passed two days on the battle-field, during which time an unhappy castle named Cavatas was knocked to bits with cannon and taken in two hours. No one was found within but some peasants, who were immediately hanged from the battlements. This example so intimidated the others, that no other places or castles resisted, with the exception of that of Pescara, the garrison of which was severely treated. Amongst others, a high steward of the manor and his son were found there; they offered a large ransom, but their offers and dignity availed them nothing, and only warranted their being hanged on the first tree. They had surrendered to a gentleman named Le Lorrain, a distinguished officer who had exchanged parole with them. He had high words with the general (the grand master) on their behalf, but, notwithstanding that, he could not save their lives.

The king took up his abode at Pescara, after he had reduced to submission the places it was his intention to overthrow—Cremona, Crème, Brescia, Bergamo, and a great number of others. The towns of Verona, Vicenza, and Padua delivered their keys to him; he sent them to the emperor, who claimed them. To the Pope, who had used him so ill, he gave Ravenna, Forli, Imola, and Faenza, in Lombardy, Brindes and Otranto, in the kingdom of Naples. He did not get much return for his generosity; the emperor soon lost his places, and the Pope became even a more dangerous enemy, as we shall shortly see.

The remnant of the Venetian army fled to Trevison and Friuli without stopping, wrongly imagining that the French were following them, at which the emperor had great reason to be satisfied.

This prince had promised the king to go to Pescara to hold a conference with him. It was agreed between them that he should come by boat down the lake which waters one side of this place, and that he should have what escort seemed good to him. The king sent the Cardinal D'Amboise to Rouvray to receive and accompany him, but this minister could not persuade him to come. The cardinal returned to the king, bringing with him the Bishop of Goritz, as the emperor's ambassador, to compliment the king and to explain the reasons why his master had not come according to his promise.

A little while after the king returned to Milan, at the commencement of July. Padua, about this time, through the carelessness of Maximilian, again fell into the hands of the Venetians. He had only left 800 lansquenets to defend the place, too small a number for a town six miles in circumference. The town was cleverly retaken by the skill of two noble Venetians, André

Gritti and Luc Malvezza, who had always had sway in this place where the Venetian dominion was dear to them, on account of the exact justice the government of the Doge gives to its subjects. These two nobles, in the commencement of July, which is in Italy the season of the second hay harvest, lay in ambush at a crossbow-shot from the town, in a place full of thick trees, which entirely obstructed the view, and concealed there without trouble 400 men-at-arms and 2000 foot-soldiers. The environs of Padua have abundance of hay, and the waggons to carry it were so large that they filled the gates of the town. Upon this they formed a design, and at break of day, the four first cartloads having entered, they had the fifth followed by six knights, each with a foot-soldier behind him armed with an arquebus, and amongst them a trumpet to sound the alarm, when the time should be come.

On the other side, the lansquenets which composed the garrison were very vigilant. They kept only two gates open, and thirty men on guard at each. The Venetian seignory had, as we have said, many spies in the town; amongst others, a gentleman named Geraldo Magurin, who was in the secret, and was to appear in arms with those of his party at the first sound of the trumpet. The fifth cartload having entered after the four others, the six men-at-arms, who followed it closely, began shouting "Marco! Marco!" The foot-soldiers behind them dismounted and fired so skilfully and closely that each one killed his man. The trumpet sounded, and the greater part of the Venetians fell upon them at once, uttering the terrible cries of "Marco! Marco! Italy! Italy!" They were seconded by Magurin, who had kept ready enough men to muster in an instant from the houses more than 2000 inhabitants armed with pikes and javelins.

The lansquenets, extremely astonished at the first charge, placed themselves promptly on the defence, and sounded the alarm; but, when they saw the general revolt, and that they must perish, they marched to the great square at once and formed a square battalion, resolved to fight vigorously and to sell their lives dearly. They had hardly formed thus when they saw themselves attacked on two or three sides at once. Such a splendid defence was never seen. They held out for two hours without breaking. In the end, the greater number conquered; they were broken and defeated without any quarter. But, in revenge, they made their conquerors pay dearly for their defeat. They killed more than 1500 on the spot, both inhabitants and assailants.

Thus the town returned to the Doge; and the Count of Pétigliano having entered, repaired and fortified it thoroughly, knowing of what importance it was to his masters.

When the emperor heard of the revolt of Padua he was furious, and swore to be avenged and go in person to punish the offenders. He asked Louis for 500 men-at-arms for three months. Louis readily agreed, and charged the brave Chabannes to choose that number from the men whose valour he could most depend upon, and take them to the emperor. Chabannes was delighted; war was his element; and as he left the gates of the castle of Milan, he met Bayard and asked him to accompany him. Bayard was as overjoyed as himself, and readily promised to do so.

These two great men gained all the victories they were trying for, and returned with great pomp to Verona, where they were magnificently received by the Bishop of Trent, for the emperor. They remained there two days, were feasted and made much of by the inhabitants, and then returned to Vicenza, which they entered readily, the people having fled as soon as they heard that the French were marching towards them. They remained five or six days at Vicenza, awaiting news of the emperor, who, they said, was already in the country; but he did not arrive till the commencement of August, when he brought with him a large number of troops, which, joined to the original French army and two reinforcements which they had recently received, made a considerable army. He received Chabannes with much pomp at the camp, near the town of Est. If they had had to wait for him, with the help of the army he had brought they soon made up for loss of time. He had with him nearly 120 princes, dukes, counts, or lords of the first German families, about 12,000 horses, and 500 or 600 lancers of Burgundy and Hainault, and nearly 50,000 infantry. Hippolite d'Est, the Cardinal of Ferrara, came to join the emperor in the name of his brother, the Duke Alphonse I, and brought 500 horses, 3000 foot-soldiers, and twelve pieces of artillery. The Cardinal of Mantua brought nearly the same number; so that altogether the army consisted of 100,000 men.

The first encampment of the emperor was at eight miles from Padua, near the palace of the Queen of Cyprus. While he was there, another reinforcement of 1000 or 1200 arrived, all picked men and fit for war, under the generalship of Jacques d'Alègre, Lord of Millaut, well worthy of commanding them. It was there that the emperor proposed the siege of Padua, and held a council of war to fix on a plan of operations. By this council it was decided that the French soldiers, with the lansquenets of the Prince of Anhalt, as the best German troop in the army, should form the point: but that, before all, it was necessary to take possession of Montselles, a little place on the road to Padua with a strong castle, whose Venetian garrison would have been able to hinder the march of the troops, and still more the convoys of provisions and ammunition.

On the morning of the next day the army set out and arrived near Montselles, which gave itself up at first, being utterly defenceless; but the castle, which was good and capable of holding out for a long time, disturbed the generals. However, by the cowardice of those who were in it, they were soon masters of it. They began to beat it down, and they had hardly commenced the breach, when the alarm was sounded for the assault. They had a good bowshot's length to climb, but the French adventurers of the Captain d'Alègre were there in so short a time that they seemed to fly. The garrison, which was entirely composed of rabble, made a show of resistance, but in a quarter of an hour the place was taken and all were massacred. The adventurers took 500 horses besides other plunder. The town and castle were given back to the Duke of Ferrara, who reclaimed them, but he had to give the emperor 30,000 ducats for them. The Cardinal d'Est took possession of it for his brother, and placed a good garrison there.

The emperor, whom we left in his camp before Montselles, had no sooner given up this place to its rightful owner, than he marched straight to Padua, and approached within a mile of it. Besides being well fortified, the city was defended by the Count of Pétigliano, a skilful general, who had with him 1000 men-at-arms, 12,000 infantry, and 200 pieces of cannon, so that raising a siege was an important matter.

The emperor encamped within a mile of the walls,

held a council of war to deliberate on which side he should form the siege, and called to it those amongst the French whom he honoured with his esteem and confidence. They agreed that the emperor should take up his position near the gate which leads to Vicenza, having the French with him; that the Cardinal of Ferrara should be at another gate higher up, with the Burgundy and Hainault soldiers and 10,000 lansquenets; that at another gate, beyond the emperor's quarters, the Cardinal of Mantua should be stationed, with his brother John and the lansquenets of the Prince of Anhalt, in order that in case of need these divisions might easily obtain help from the main body of the army.

Bayard, for whom the most perilous tasks were always reserved, was ordered to go. first, accompanied by the young Bussy d'Amboise, La Cropte-Daillon, La Clayette, &c. Now there was a high road, perfectly straight, going right to the gate of Vicenza, upon which, at a distance of 200 feet, they had constructed four large barriers furnished with men and firearms; and on each side this road was bordered with wide and deep ditches, according to the custom of Italy, in order that they might only be attacked from the front. They placed artillerymen on the walls of the town which overlooked the road, and which, over the barriers, and without inconveniencing those who guarded them, fired upon the French a hail-storm of cannon.

In the meantime Bayard and his companions attacked the first barrier, which was well defended; nevertheless, they managed to force it, and drove the enemy to the second. If the fight was hot at the first, it was hotter still at the second barrier. Young Bussy had his arm pierced with a shot, and his horse killed under

him; but he did not leave the party on that account;
on the contrary, he became more furious. At this
second attack the Captain d'Alègre came to their aid
with 120 of his chosen men, who were more like lions
than men. All this happened at mid-day, so that it was
easy to see who did his duty and who neglected it.
After half an hour's fighting, the second barrier was
forced and taken, and the enemy were chased and pursued so closely that they could not remain at the third,
and were happy to be able to reach the fourth. This
was at a stone's throw from the ramparts of the town,
and guarded by 1000 or 1200 men, with three or four
falconets, which made a terrible fire upon the main
road, but (incredible fact) only killed two horses. The
fugitives, who had joined themselves at the barrier with
those who guarded it, took courage under shelter of the
walls of the place, and the attack having lasted an hour,
Bayard was tired of such a lengthy resistance, and
cried to his men, "Comrades, this is lasting too long;
let us dismount and force the barrier." They did so,
to the number of thirty or forty, and, with visor raised
and lance lowered, they rushed upon the Venetian
guard. Near Bayard fought the Prince d'Anhalt, Jean
le Picard, and the Captain Maulevrier, who all fought
furiously. But Bayard, seeing that the enemy was
momentarily reinforced, cried out a second time, "Comrades, they shall keep us here as long as they like. Let
us give them assault. Follow me, all of you; sound
trumpet." He himself led the way with the fury of a
lion. His companions seconded him so well that the
enemy withdrew a pike's length. Then Bayard, without
hesitation, leapt over the barrier, shouting, "Friends,
they are ours! let us go on!" Those who had dismounted vaulted after him, and those who had remained

on horseback, seeing the danger in which their comrades were, imitated them in crying "France! France! Empire! Empire!" Then the attack went on with redoubled force, and was such that the enemy left the place, and fled in disorder into the town. Thus the four barriers were forced, in open day, to the great glory of the French, and especially of our hero, to whom all unanimously gave the honour. This expedition over, the artillery was immediately brought down to the bank of the moat, and the soldiers were so quartered that they formed three camps, as had been previously arranged. The army and its followers were so numerous that they covered an area of more than four miles, in a country so abundant in provisions, corn, wine, and hay, and everything necessary for both men and horses, that at the raising of the siege, which lasted about two months and a half, they burnt the worth of 100,000 ducats which they could not carry away.

The day after the taking of the barriers the artillery began their work, and commenced their terrible fire, which the town returned with usury. They made three breaches, which were speedily converted into one, and consequently more than large enough for an assault.

While the artillery were at work, one of the emperor's cannoneers was discovered firing against the camp, instead of the town. His trial was soon finished. He was placed in a mortar instead of a bomb, and blown to bits towards the town. They accused one of the emperor's generals of this treason, a Greek, named Constantine, who governed the emperor, and was the cause of his committing great faults; yet he was his favourite. They suspected him of having corrupted this man, and even of being concerned in a plot with the Count of Pétigliano, giving him news of everything that happened in the emperor's camp. Chabannes reproached him publicly, treated him as a traitor and a coward, and challenged him to fight; but the other refused, saying his conscience would not allow it. The emperor, to prevent ill consequences, reconciled them.

The Count of Pétigliano, whether he had been told or not, had fortified his place so well, that 500,000 men could not carry it. He had made behind the breach a moat, with ditches twenty feet deep and as many wide, where he had put several layers of fagots and dry wood, all covered with gunpowder, and at a hundred steps apart he had raised a rampart with artillery, which commanded the whole length of the moat. Beside this insurmountable trench was a beautiful esplanade, where the Venetian army, cavalry and infantry, could range themselves in battle, to the number of 20,000 men, and behind this esplanade he had raised platforms, furnished with from twenty to thirty pieces of cannon each, pointed to the breach over the heads of the garrison. When some French officers fell into the hands of the Count of Pétigliano, made prisoner in skirmishes, and who ransomed themselves, they made no difficulty of letting them see these entrenchments, that they should give an account of them to their generals, especially to Chabannes, and inform him of the certain danger of hazarding the assault. "For," he said to them on taking leave, "I hope that the republic will get sooner or later into the good graces of the King of France, and if it were not for the consideration that I have for your nation, and those who are with the emperor, I assure you that I would make him raise the siege to-morrow." All that was reported to the French generals, but the king, having given them to the emperor for auxiliaries, they would not take anything upon themselves. Before we relate what the emperor intended to do, we may note two adventures that befel our hero.

During the siege of Padua, the besieged frequently inconvenienced the emperor by their attacks. The garrison of Trévisa, another good place twenty or twenty-five miles from there, served him the same. It was commanded by the Duke of Malvezze, an excellent captain, and by other officers. This commander did not fail to give the alert to the imperial camp two or three times a week, and when he found an occasion, he profited by it; if, on the contrary, he found resistance, he retired. He continued this manœuvre a long time, but so wisely, that he never lost a single one of his men. Bayard was tired of this, and said to two of his particular friends, with whom he lodged, La Cropte-Daillon and La Clayette, "This Captain Malvezze," said he, "is too much talked about. I am sorry he does not know what sort of men we are. If you will second me, we will look for him to-morrow, and as he has not appeared for two days, I do not despair of finding him."

Bayard had spies, whom he paid so well that they would not have betrayed him at the peril of their lives. One of them had informed him of the route and the forces of Malvezze. Having arranged his plans upon this information, and his two friends having consented to join him, he told each of them to arm thirty brave men-at-arms, at two o'clock in the morning; and "I," added he, "will take my company with some of our good companions, Bonnet, Mipont, Cossé, Brezon, and others, and we will mount in the strictest silence. Confide in me, I have a guide in whom I can trust." At two o'clock in the morning, in the month of September, all were on horseback, and the spy walked before, escorted by four soldiers. Bayard, too prudent to place himself entirely in the power of such men without precaution, had promised him a large reward if he did his duty; but in case of treason, the four soldiers had orders to kill him with their poniards. This spy served him well, and led the company for about ten miles. When day broke, they found themselves near a large and beautiful country house, an extensive garden, and a park surrounded by walls. The spy pointed it out to Bayard, and assured him that if this was the day upon which Captain Malvezze had to give the alarm to the camp, he would necessarily pass there; that as this castle was abandoned on account of the war, it was easy for the soldiers to lie in ambush there, seeing all, but unseen themselves. The advice was considered good. They entered the castle, and remained for two hours, without results. At the end of that time, they heard a great noise of horses, which was just what they had been awaiting.

Bayard had with him an old soldier, named Monart, an experienced warrior, and a man in whom he could place implicit trust. He had placed him as sentinel in the dove-cote of the house, to examine whom and how many they had to deal with. This soldier saw from a distance, and recognized the Captain Malvezze, with his troop, which he judged to consist of about 100 men-at-arms, and about 200 Albanians, commanded by the Captain Scanderbeg, all well mounted, and with the air of men ready for anything. This troop having passed the French ambuscade about a bow-shot, the sentinel went down, and made his report, at which everyone was pleased. Then Bayard ordered them to harness their horses, which each one did himself, because they had no grooms with them. Then he said to his company: "Friends, it is ten years since such a good adventure came in our way, and if each of us do his duty, the number ought not to astonish us; they are two against one, but that is very trifling. Let us set out immediately." All having answered, " Let us go ! let us set out!" the gate was opened, and they galloped briskly after their enemies. After having marched a mile, they discovered them on the high road, and Bayard ordered the trumpet to sound. The Venetians, much astonished at hearing the trumpet, thought it must be some of their own men coming to join them. Nevertheless, they waited to know, and were much deceived. To their surprise was joined the fear of finding themselves shut in between the advancing enemy and the emperor's camp, without any possible means of escape ; but they took courage again when they saw the few men approaching.

The Captain Malvezze encouraged his men, exhorted them to do well, because they must conquer or perish ; that there remained no means of escape, the road being bordered by fosses so deep and wide that no knight would have the boldness to jump them. Afterwards, he had the trumpet sounded, and the French trumpet answered. When they were a bow-shot the one from the other, they began to charge, the French crying, " France ! France ! Empire ! Empire !" and the Spaniards, " Marco! Marco!" The first charge was severe. A great number were unsaddled. The Captain Bonnet pierced a gendarme through and through with one stroke of his lance, and on both sides the fight was very desperate. The Albanians left their soldiers with the French, and, thinking to surprise them from behind, they went off the high road. Bayard perceived this, and said to La Cropte-Daillon, " Keep your eye upon them, so that they do not shut us in. I will undertake those who are before us." La Cropte did so, and when the Albanians thought to fall upon the French, they were so well received that a dozen of them were left on the field, and the rest took to flight, and departed as fast as their legs could carry them. La Cropte did not pursue them. He returned to the main body; but the action was finished, the Venetians were conquered, and the victors were already seizing their prisoners. The Captain Malvezze, with twenty or thirty of the best mounted, crossed the moat, and returned whence they came. The French did not pursue them; their horses went too fast, owing to the vigorous spurring of their masters.

The French began the retreat with more prisoners than men; but they deprived them of their swords, and made them march in the midst, and in this manner they reached the camp. Just at this juncture the emperor was walking with some of his courtiers; and perceiving a thick cloud of dust, he sent a French officer, Louis de Peschin, to learn the meaning of it. This officer told him that the captains Bayard, La Cropte, and La Clayette, had returned from performing the boldest stroke that the last 100 years had witnessed. The emperor could not conceal his joy. He visited the troop, and complimented them generally, and he congratulated each captain upon such a day; and finally, addressing himself to Bayard, he said, "Knight, the king, my brother and your master, is proud and happy to have such a man as you in his service. I wish I had a dozen like you, if they cost me 100,000 florins a year."

CHAPTER VII.

NO previous expedition ever made so much stir as this, and no captain ever got so much honour as Bayard; but, with his accustomed modesty, he attributed the glory to his friends and soldiers, and never to himself.

A few days after this action, he learnt from his spies that Captain Scanderbeg, with his Albanians and some other horsemen, had retired into the Castle of Bassano, and that from there they made raids upon those who came to the camp, and upon the foot-soldiers who were returning to Germany with their booty and horses that they had taken from the enemy; and that in a few days even they had defeated more than 200, and retaken from them four or five hundred oxen or cows, which they had with them in the castle; "and if you like," added the spy, "I can take you to a defile at the foot of a mountain where they will fall into your hands." Bayard, who had always found this man faithful, and had always paid him well, resolved to follow him, without informing any one of his intention, feeling certain that with his thirty men-at-arms, his company of archers, and ten or twelve gentlemen who were attached to him, and who served as volunteers simply to learn the art of war from him, he could easily defeat 200 light-horse Albanians, who had for a chief Renault Contarini, a noble Venetian, a native of Padua. He informed his soldiers and friends of his plan, who were charmed with it. Everything being ready, they set out an hour before daybreak, one Saturday in the month of September, and travelled fifteen miles with their spy, before arriving at the defile, where they were fortunate enough to arrive without being seen. They ambuscaded themselves at a cannon-shot from the castle, and a moment afterwards they heard a trumpet, which from the castle sounded "To horse." Bayard, very pleased with his expedition, asked the spy what road he thought the Albanians would take. He replied, "that whatever road they took, they must necessarily pass a little wooden bridge, which was at a mile from there, and which two men could easily guard; and when they have passed," added he, "send some of your men to seize the bridge, so that they cannot return, and I will conduct you by a gorge which I know of in the mountains to a plain near the palace of the Queen of Cyprus, where you will surely meet them." It was then merely a question as to who should guard the bridge. The Lord of Bonnet said, "Captain, if you have no objection, Mipont and I will guard the bridge, with as many men as you shall see fit to give us." Bayard consented, and gave them six men-at-arms, and ten or twelve archers.

Whilst they were making these arrangements, they heard the noise of the Albanian troop coming down from the castle, as if they were going to a wedding, reckoning upon making some good capture, according to custom; but they had reckoned too surely this time.

They let them pass the bridge, and immediately Bonnet and his companions seized it, whilst Bayard and his men followed the spy into the defile of the mountain.

They were so well conducted that in less than half an hour they found themselves in a plain where they would have seen a knight at 6,000 steps. Then they saw, at something more than a cannon-shot from them, their enemies, who were taking the road to Vicenza, where they reckoned upon an encounter with the enemy. Bayard ordered his standard-bearer, the bastard Du Fay, to take twenty men, and to go and skirmish, to engage them in action, and then to fly, as if frightened at so large a number. "Bring them here," said he, " I await you at the foot of the mountain, and you shall see some fine sport." Du Fay did not wait to say more; he saw the whole plan at a glance. He then went near enough to the enemies to be recognized by his white crosses. Then Scanderbeg and his men, overjoyed at the meeting, began the charge, crying "Marco!" Du Fay, pretending great fear, fled with all his might, accompanied by his men, towards the mountain, and were pursued so hotly that the enemies precipitated themselves into the ambuscade of Bayard, who awaited them fully prepared. He immediately appeared with his men, who, like so many lions, fell upon the enemy, crying "Empire! France!" and at the first shock they unsaddled more than thirty men. The Albanians and the crossbowmen kept up some time, but finally they galloped off in the direction of the bridge by which they had crossed an hour previously. They were so well-mounted that Bayard would have lost his prey if the bridge had not been guarded by Bonnet, Mipont, and their men, who hindered their crossing by it. This second surprise put Scanderbeg under the necessity of fighting or flying. The greater number adopted the latter plan: but they were so well followed that they took from them two captains, thirty crossbowmen, and sixty Albanians. The rest escaped across country to Trevisa.

A few days before, Bayard had received as a cadet into his company a young gentleman of Dauphiny, named Guignes Geoffrey, son of the Lord of Boutières; he was between sixteen and seventeen years old; and, being descended from brave ancestors, he was already capable of walking in their steps. He was in this expedition of Bayard's, and he gave good promise of what he would do in the future. Having seen the standard-bearer of Contarini leap a ditch and take to flight during the action, he vaulted after him at the risk of breaking his neck, and soon reached him. He gave him such a sudden and powerful blow with his lance that he shivered it to pieces, and upset the fugitive; then, taking his sword in his hand, he cried, "Yield yourself, sir ensign, or I will kill you." Preferring the former to the latter course, the ensign gave his sword and flag into the boy's hands. Geoffrey, more overjoyed than if he had found his weight in gold, made him remount his horse, and march before him to the place where he had left Bayard. He arrived as they were sounding retreat, and saw so many prisoners that he was embarrassed. Bonnet was the first who perceived him, and who showed him to the knight, returning with his prisoner and flag. Bayard never felt more pleased in his life. "Have you taken this standard-bearer and his flag?" he asked. "Yes, sir," replied Geoffrey; "God has given me that favour; but I assure you, if he had not given himself up, I should have killed him." This speech doubled the pleasure of Bayard and the whole assembled company, and he said to him, "Boutières, my dear friend, you have begun well; God grant that you may continue;" which the result verified, for he became an excellent officer.

Our hero, not content with the expedition just recorded, still wished to make himself master of the castle of Bassano. He spoke of it to his companions, Bonnet, Mipont, and Pierrepont, his nephew and lieutenant, and other officers who had followed him. "For," said he, "they have that within that will enrich our men." "That is more easily said than done," they replied. "Remember the castle is strong, and we have no artillery." "For my part," answered Bayard, "I intend to have it in a quarter of an hour." He then had the two Venetian Captains, Contarini and Scanderbeg brought before him, and said to them: "Gentlemen, I know it is in your power to put me in instant possession of the castle; I give you your choice to do so, or to have your heads cut off before its gates presently." They promised to do their best; and indeed, he who commanded there, a nephew of Scanderbeg's, gave it up as soon as his uncle had asked him.

They found there more than five hundred oxen and cows, and a quantity of plunder; the whole was equally distributed among the victorious troops, who were greatly enriched by it. The cattle were led to Vicenza, where each one received the value of his share in money. They found in the castle plenty of provisions for their horses, and sufficient to make good cheer for themselves. They made their two prisoners sit down to table with them; and at the end of the meal young Boutières entered to salute his captain, and to present his prisoner, who was a man of thirty years, twice as big as he was.

At the sight of this disproportion Bayard could not help laughing; then, addressing himself to the two Venetians: "Gentlemen," said he, "here is a child who only six days ago was a page, and who will not have a beard for three years; nevertheless he has taken your flag; what do you say to it? I don't know what your officers think of it, but we French are less easily overcome; it requires some trouble for stronger than we to wrest our flag from us."

The Venetian ensign felt how humiliating this pleasantry was to him, and he replied, in his own tongue, "My faith, captain, if I gave myself up, it was not because I was afraid of the boy who took me; he could not have made me prisoner; but I could not resist the whole troop."

Bayard at this answer looked at Boutières, and said to him, "Do you hear what your prisoner has just said?" The young man, cut to the quick, reddened with vexation, and begged the knight to grant him a favour he had to ask. Having obtained it, he said, "Sir, it is that you will allow me to give back his arms and horse to this man, and to get upon my own; we will go together to the meadow and fight once more; if he conquers I give him back his ransom, but if I am victorious I swear to him before God that I will kill him."

"Certainly, I grant you what you wish," cried Bayard, joyfully; but the Venetian would not run the risk, and shamefully refused the challenge; thus Boutières had the honour of a second victory.

After they had dined, the French resumed their homeward route, taking with them their prisoners. They were received as well as they had been on the former occasion. Bayard was congratulated by the emperor himself; but young Boutières carried off the palm, both for the capture of the Venetian ensign, and the offer he had made to give him his revenge. Chabannes especially could not sufficiently admire him, and told him that he was a worthy representative of the house of Geoffrey, which he had known a long time, and which had always been fruitful in great men.

We must now return to the siege of Padua, where we left the emperor resolved to commence the assault. This prince, seeing the success of the artillery, and that one of the three breaches was 500 feet wide, reproached himself for his weakness, in not having commenced sooner, considering the number and strength of his army. He had hardly returned to his quarters with the lords and princes of his court, when he sent for a secretary to whom he dictated the following letter to Chabannes, who was lodged quite near to him :—

"My cousin, I have been this morning to see the breach of the town, which I consider easily got through by him who wishes to do his duty. I have appointed the assault for to-day. I therefore pray you that as soon as my great drum sounds, which will be about midday, you shall hold ready all the French gentlemen under your command, at my service, by the order of my brother the King of France, to go to the said assault with my foot-soldiers, and I hope, with God's help, that we shall carry the place."

The same secretary who had written the letter was ordered to carry it to Chabannes, who considered the emperor's proposition very extraordinary; however, he contented himself with replying to the secretary that he was exceedingly surprised that the emperor had not done his brother officers and himself the honour of calling them together to deliberate upon an affair of such importance, and he also charged him to tell his imperial majesty, that he would call the officers together and communicate to them the contents of his letter, and he had no doubt that they would be ready to obey him.

When the secretary had departed, Chabannes sent word to all the captains to assemble themselves at his quarters. The report had already spread that the assault would be made on that day, and it was a curious thing to see each soldier anxious to confess himself, paying for his turn with a good heavy sum of gold, some of the men even trusting their purses to the priests who confessed them. The historian adds that there was never so much money before seen with an army, and he has no doubt that the reverend gentlemen would not have been displeased if they who entrusted their money to them had fallen in the assault and remained in the breach. Besides the abundance of specie, that of provisions was not less; and not a day passed but three or four hundred lansquenets deserted, taking away to their country all sorts of animals, furniture, clothes, and other articles; so much so that they valued the plunder taken in the domain of Padua at two million crowns, including the cost of burnt palaces and houses.

When all the captains had arrived, Chabannes ordered dinner to be served, "Because," said he, laughing, "I have something to say to you presently which might take away your appetites." He well knew what sort of men he was talking to, and that in the whole company there was not one man who was not a hero, especially Bayard, whose right to that title no one disputed. The meal ended, all but the French officers went out. Then Chabannes read them the emperor's letter, and read it again so that they might thoroughly understand it. The surprise was so great that they looked at each other, each apparently expecting the other to speak. Humbercourt broke silence, and said, laughingly, that the Lord of Chabannes could send word to the emperor that they were all disposed to obey him. " I begin," said he, "to get tired of this; moreover we're getting to the bottom of our good wine."

They smiled at this sally, and everyone said his say,

agreeing with Humbercourt. Bayard alone said nothing, and seemed absent-minded, sitting still and picking his teeth.

"What do you say, O Hercules of France?" Chabannes asked, good humouredly, "is this a time for picking teeth? What answer shall we make to the emperor?"

Bayard, who never lost his good humour, replied in the same tone, "If we all wish to follow the advice of the Lord D'Humbercourt, we have only to go straight to the breach; but as it is not the business of a man-at-arms to fight on foot, I could willingly dispense with the honour. In the meantime, I will tell you my opinion upon the subject, as you wish to know. The emperor commands you to make foot-soldiers of all the French gentlemen, that they may go to the breach with the lansquenets: as for me, although I have neither wealth nor lordship, I have the honour of being a gentleman. I do not compare myself to you, my lords, who are all rich and of great houses, as nearly all my company are; but I don't know what the emperor is thinking of in wishing to compromise so much nobility with his foot-soldiers, of whom one is a shoemaker, another a baker, another a tailor; and, besides, they are men who have no previously gained glory to recommend them, as we have; begging his majesty's pardon, it is degrading us too much. This, my lord," added he, "is what I think you should answer:—You have assembled your captains together; they are determined to follow his orders, as far as they agree with those of the king their master; that he cannot be ignorant that the king has none but gentlemen under his orders, and it is too much to underrate them by mixing them with his foot-soldiers; but that he has a number of counts, German lords and gentlemen, that he can put on foot with the French men-at-arms, to whom we will show the way; and that after that he can send his lansquenets to get a taste of it, and see how they like it."

When he had finished this speech, every one agreed with him, without exception. The answer was then put into shape, and sent to the emperor, who appeared pleased with it. Immediately he had trumpets and drums sounded to assemble the princes, captains, and lords of his court and his army, as well of Germany as of Burgundy and Flanders. He declared to them that he was resolved to give the assault in an hour; that he had warned the French lords and captains of it, who all promised to do their duty, but had begged that the German gentlemen should go with them, they willingly marching first to the breach. "That is why," added he, "I entreat you all in my power to accept the part, and to go on foot with them; and I hope, at the first assault, we shall carry the place."

This speech finished, murmurings were heard amongst the Germans for the space of nearly half an hour. Finally, one of the best qualified, deputed to speak for the rest, told the emperor that their duty was to fight on horseback, like gentlemen, and not on foot; still less did it become them to go to a breach. The emperor could scarcely expect any other answer, and though he was extremely displeased, he hid his vexation, and only said to them, "It will be necessary, then, to consult as to what is best to be done." He immediately sent for a gentleman of his household, named Rocandolff, who was ordinarily charged with his commissions for the generals, and who was as often with them as with his master, and said, "Go from me to my cousin, the Lord of La Palisse; commend me to him and all the French lords with him, and tell him that there will be no assault to-day." This answer having been taken to Chabannes, everyone disarmed himself, some glad, others sorry, for there were some among them, says the historian,[1] who had reckoned otherwise. The emperor showed great self-possession in disguising from his nobility the vexation he felt when they refused the service which the French undertook, but he was not the less piqued.

---

[1] The people who were displeased at this result were evidently the reverend depositaries of the soldiers' money, "Certes," adds the Loyal Servant, "the priests were not overdelighted, they being obliged to restore what had been delivered into their keeping." The emperor removed after this more than forty miles from the camp, and ordered the siege to be raised.

CHAPTER VIII.

THE valiant Prince of Anhalt thought differently to the others; he not only told the emperor of his willingness to go to the breach, but he went again to find the French, and to show them how discontented he was at what had happened. There was with him in the imperial army an officer distinguished by his bravery, and all sorts of good qualities, who was called Jacob Emps, or Empser, a gentleman of Swabia, in the diocese of Constance, and who in the end passed into the king's service. He often made one of the French party when there were assaults or skirmishes to be made. But this Captain Jacob and the Prince of Anhalt could not make up for all the Germans. The emperor played a very singular part, suggested by the indignation that his officers had caused him. He left his army the following night very secretly, escorted by a body-guard of 500 or 600 men, and retired to his own estates, forty miles distant. Thence he sent to Constantine, his lieutenant-general, and to the Lord of Palisse, to raise the siege as well as they could under the circumstances.

The sudden departure of this prince equally surprised

his own soldiers and the French. In the meantime, pursuant to his orders, they held a council of war, and resolved upon raising the siege. It was not a very easy operation to transport about 140 pieces of cannon; there were only carriages for about half the number. The French were ordered to escort them, and by their means this numerous artillery was all removed. But the Prince of Anhalt, to cover the shame of his nation as much as possible, did not leave the escort during the whole process of removal, and he was on foot and armed from morning till evening, without giving himself time to eat, which acquired him the honour and esteem of the French.

They practised the same manœuvre for taking many cannon that they had recourse to on their arrival: they took part of them, and returned with the carriages to take others, and so on till all were carried there. In the meantime, the garrison of Padua made vigorous sallies from hour to hour, notwithstanding which the siege was raised without the loss of a single man by either army. The German lansquenets burnt every house that they left, and all they found on their road. Bayard, who had a horror of excess, and of everything contrary to the laws of war, made seven or eight of his men remain in a beautiful house, which he had occupied, until after the departure of the German savages, and by that means preserved it from burning.

The armies arrived, after several days' march, at Vicenza, where Chabannes received letters from the emperor and presents for him and the other French captains, according to the power of that prince, who was much more generous than rich. He had good qualities, but they were obscured by an essential defect, which affected his whole life: he persisted in defying the whole world, and planning alone, and without advice, all his enterprises.

The armies separated at Vicenza. The Germans took the road to their country, excepting one garrison, which remained in the town, commanded by the Lord of Reu. The French army retired into the Milanais on All Saints' Day, and Bayard remained in garrison at Verona, where he signalized himself by new exploits against the Venetians, who then held a little place in the neighbourhood, named Lignago, whence they made sallies into the country. During his sojourn at Verona, where he had only 200 or 300 French men-at-arms in the service of the emperor, those who guarded Vicenza for that prince did not believe themselves in safety. Besides that they were weak themselves, they were still threatened with a siege; they withdrew to Verona, near the knight, where, only finding a moderate garrison, they passed beyond, and encamped fifteen or eighteen miles farther off, at a village named St. Boniface. The winter began to make itself felt, and Bayard's people were obliged to leave their place to find forage, and sometimes go to a great distance—so much so, that he was obliged to have them escorted, because from time to time he lost grooms and horses in encounters with the enemy.

The Venetians had a brave and enterprising captain, who annoyed the French every day by making inroads to the very gates of Verona. Bayard resolved to meet him and moderate his ardour. For that reason he wished himself to escort the first foraging party, and to see close this Venetian, named John Paul Manfroni. Manfroni, informed of Bayard's design by a spy who was near him, wished to profit by the occasion, and to take sufficient men with him to be the stronger party, and give the knight the worst of it.

One day the foragers, having set out from Verona, supported by thirty or forty men-at-arms or archers, commanded by the Captain Pierrepont, went towards the country houses to forage. The knight, who believed himself master of his secret, was concealed, with 100 men-at-arms, in a village named St. Martin, on the high road from Verona, and about six miles from it. He sent scouts out to reconnoitre, who soon returned with the news that they had seen the enemy, to the number of 500 horse, drawing up right where the foragers were. Manfroni, warned by his spy of Bayard's intention, and of the number of his men, had concealed five or six hundred men in a deserted palace, pike men and arquebusiers, and had told them what to do, especially not to appear until they saw him fly, and the French after him. He could not form his plans better than to surround them, and thus put them between two fires.

As soon as Bayard learnt of the arrival of the enemy's troops, he ordered his own to horse, without being in the least afraid of the disproportion. He had not gone two miles when he discovered them, and marching straight forward to charge them, crying "France!" and "Empire!" They kept firm a moment, but on the approach of the French they pretended to retreat, marching backwards towards the ambuscade, which they passed at about 100 feet distant, always appearing to defend themselves; then they stopped suddenly, and began crying, "Marco! Marco!" At this signal the foot soldiers emerged from their ambuscade and fired upon the French. Bayard's horse was killed at the first discharge, and he fell heavily, with one leg under the animal. Immediately his men-at-arms, who would have given their lives to save his, surrounded him, and one of them, named Grandmont, dismounted and disengaged him.

But however good their defence, they could not hinder Bayard and Grandmont from being taken prisoners by some foot-soldiers, who wished to deprive them of their arms. Pierrepont, who was with the foragers, hearing the noise, put his horse to the gallop, and arrived as the two prisoners were already out of the ranks to be taken away. At sight of this fury seized him; he fell like a lion upon those who guarded them, and by furious sword blows obliged them to release their prey and to fly towards their troop, which was engaged with the French, and both sides fought well.

Bayard and Grandmont, remounted, ran to the help of their men, who were sorely pressed both in front and in the rear, but at the sight of their captain and Pierrepont they regained courage. However, the inequality was too great; the Venetians were ten to one, without taking into account the inconvenience that the arquebusiers caused the French. Bayard felt the danger, and said to his nephew Pierrepont, "Captain, if we do not gain the high road we shall perish here, and if we can reach it we shall escape in spite of them, and, God helping us, without loss." "I think with you," replied Pierrepont, and they began to retire towards the high road, which they finally reached with the greatest difficulty, fighting every step of the way. They had, however, unsaddled seven or eight horsemen, and put an end to forty or fifty of the foot-soldiers, without losing one of their own men.

When Bayard and his troop had gained the high road they formed a square, always fighting as they retired, and now and then turning upon their enemies, to whom they gave some trouble; but they had on their flank foot-soldiers, whose arquebuses inconvenienced them much. The knight again had his horse wounded under him; feeling it stagger he dismounted, and performed prodigies of valour, without any other arms than his sword. He was obliged, however, to yield to numbers. He was already surrounded, when the bastard Du Fay, his standard-bearer, came with his archers, and fell upon the Venetians with so much bravery and success that he took him out of their hands, and re-mounted him in spite of them. Then, again forming a square squadron, they regained the high road to the town with the honour of the day and that of having fought against a number ten times as large as their own, of having dismounted a number of their enemies, and only lost a single man.

As the night was coming on, Bayard ordered that the charge should cease, and that they should retire towards St. Martin, whence they had set out at the commencement of the day. He ordered a halt on a bridge furnished with barriers, to see if they would not be followed. But the Captain Manfroni, seeing that they were out of his reach, and that they might receive help from Verona, beat a retreat, and gave orders for taking the road to St. Boniface. He made the foot soldiers defile before him; but they were overcome with fatigue, having fought for four or five hours without pause. They wished to remain at a village four or five miles from St. Boniface, in spite of their captain, who was forced to leave them there, and to continue his route with his horse soldiers. Manfroni was in a very ill temper at the treatment they had received at the hands of so small a body of men.

Bayard and his troop passed the night at St. Martin, where they found plenty with which to make good cheer, and to make up for the fatigue of the day. They congratulated each other upon their happy escape from the danger in which they had been placed, and with so little loss, only having lost one archer and four horses.

During the supper a spy of Bayard's arrived, coming from St. Boniface. When he was brought in, the knight asked him what the enemy was about; the spy replied that they were in great numbers at St. Boniface, and that they boasted that soon they should take Verona, by means of the intelligence that they had received. "But as I went out," added he, "the Captain Manfroni arrived there, very much fatigued, and still more vexed, for I heard him say that he had come from the skirmish, where he had been fighting with devils, and not men. And at four or five miles from here," said the spy, " I passed through a village full of their foot-soldiers, who are staying there, and who appeared to me very much fatigued." "I wager my head," said Bayard, " that they are those we saw to-day, and that they are so fatigued with their day's work that they have not been able to go farther. If you are willing, comrades, they shall be ours. We will have our horses well fed, and towards four o'clock in the morning we will go by moonlight and wake them up." All were of his opinion, and after having had their horses well groomed, and ordered the watch, everyone went to rest excepting Bayard, who never slept when he had the idea of an expedition in his head. He was on horseback by three o'clock in the morning with his troop. Silently they took the road to the village that the spy pointed out, and on their arrival they found neither watch nor sentinel. They began their ordinary cry, "Empire! France! To the death! to the death!" The sleepers awoke at the noise, and still half asleep, came out of the houses, and found outside men ready to slaughter them like beasts. Their captain assembled two or three hundred men, thinking they would be able to defend themselves, but his opponents did not give him time; he was charged so vigorously that he and two brothers only were left of all of them. The two brothers were exchanged for two French gentlemen, prisoners of the Republic.

When Bayard had so gloriously ended this double expedition, he thought he ought not to risk losing the fruit of it by any check, so he returned to Verona, where he was triumphantly received. The Venetians, on the contrary, were enraged at the second defeat of their men, and the provéditore André Gritti wanted to lay the blame on the Captain Manfroni, who justified himself well, but meditated having his revenge with as little delay as possible.

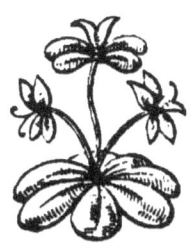

CHAPTER IX.

SEVEN or eight days after the massacre of the Venetian foot-soldiers, this Captain Manfroni bargained with a spy, who was employed by Bayard and himself, went from one to the other, and took money from both; and yet was better affected towards Manfroni than Bayard. Manfroni thus instructed him: " Go to Verona, and make the Captain Bayard understand that the senate has nominated the present commander at Lignago to go to the Levant with the state galleys; that the provéditore has orders to send me in his place to Lignago, and that you know for a certainty that I shall start for my destination tomorrow at daybreak with 300 light horse, and no foot-soldiers. I know his high spirit too well to doubt that he will allow the opportunity to escape of visiting me on my journey; and if he comes, I promise you that the best that can happen to him will be to be taken prisoner; for I shall put 200 men-at-arms and 2000 foot-soldiers in L'Isola della Scala, in ambush; and if you fulfil my commission well, I promise you, on my honour as a gentleman, 200 golden ducats."

The spy, dazzled by such a large sum, promised to do his duty, and went to Verona the same day. He went straight to Bayard's quarters, where he was well known to the servants, who saw him often, and believed him faithful to their master. They took him to him while he was still at supper, and he was better received than he deserved.

"Vicentin," said Bayard to him, "you do not come for nothing: what news?"

"Good news, sir," he replied. At these words Bayard left the table and drew him aside. The false spy told him his commission with so much apparent faith that Bayard was as glad as he could possibly be. He ordered supper for his informant and feasted him well; then he called the Captains Pierrepont, Du Fay, La Varrenne, who then bore his flag, and the Lord of Sucker, a Burgundian gentleman, who had supped with them, and told them word for word what he had just heard of the movements of the Captain Manfroni, that he was to be at Lignago the next day with only 300 horse. He asked them if they were in the humour to follow him, saying that the day should not pass till Manfroni had been well punished. Everyone being willing, they agreed at once to set out at daybreak with 200 men-at-arms, and sent word to the Lord of Conti (Frederick de Mailly), and made him promise to be ready by a given time. He had no thought of refusing, he liked the business too well, especially in Bayard's company. Then they separated to get themselves ready to assemble in good time. Thus would they have gone blindly to destruction if Providence had not saved them. The Lord of Sucker, who lodged at a good distance from Bayard, returning to his own quarters, saw the same spy leaving a house which he suspected; it was occupied by a noble Veronese, known to be more Venetian than imperial. Sucker took the spy by the collar and asked him where he had come from. The spy, taken by surprise, excused himself so badly that he only increased the suspicions of his unfaithfulness. The captain, without releasing his hold, returned to Bayard dragging the spy with him. Our hero was about to retire for the night; he, however, ordered the spy to be put in security, and then Sucker told him what had happened, that he had seen this man come from the house of the Seigneur Voltège, the most suspected partisan of the republic in the town, that in his surprise he had changed colour, and stammered, and not been able to justify himself.

Bayard, on hearing this, did not doubt for an instant that treason was on foot. He sent for the spy, and asked him what he had been doing at Voltège's house. The coward replied at first that he had a relation in the house; then he gave another excuse; finally, he contradicted himself five or six times. They brought handcuffs to make him explain more clearly, and Bayard had the goodness to promise him, on the faith of a gentleman, that no harm should happen to him although he had conspired against the knight's life, provided he told the whole truth, but that if he did not he should be hanged at break of day.

The spy, seeing that he could no longer dissimulate, threw himself on his knees before the knight, and begged for mercy; then he confessed the plan of Captain Manfroni to surprise him in an ambuscade of 200 men-at-arms, and 2000 foot-soldiers in L'Isola della Scala; that he had been to Voltège to inform him of it, and to know of him how he could some night give up one of the gates of the town to the Provéditore André Gritti, and many other things besides; but that Voltège had declared he would enter into no treason, and that as the emperor had become his master he wished to keep faith with him. When he had finished his confession Bayard said to him calmly, "Vicentin, I have employed to very bad purpose the ducats I have given you, and though I have always looked upon you as a rascal, you are far worse than I should have believed you—you richly deserve death, but as I have given you my word that I will not take your life, I will keep faith, and have you put in safety out of the town, but beware of entering it again, for the whole world shall not prevent my hanging you if you do." At these words he drove him from his presence and had him shut up in a room to await further orders.

Bayard, left alone with the Captain Sucker, said to him, "What can we do to repay Captain Manfroni for the good turn he intended us? We must have our revenge, and if you will do what I tell you, believe me we shall soon be quits with him."

"You have only to speak," replied the captain, "I am ready to do anything."

"Go then at once," said Bayard, "to the Prince of Anhalt, present my compliments to him, and give him an exact account of this affair; beg him to give us 2000 lansquenets to-morrow, whom we will take with us to a good place, and, if you do not see wonders, never believe me again."

The Captain Sucker fulfilled Bayard's commission, and the prince, who loved him, and esteemed his valour, granted his request immediately, saying that Bayard was as much master of his troops as he was himself or more so, and that he wished he could be one of the party. Then he sent his secretary with his orders to four or five captains, who were ready with their companies as soon as those who had been warned in the evening.

The Baron of Conti, who did not know what had

happened, was astonished at the number; but when he was informed of the plot by Bayard, "On my faith," said he, "we shall have a merry day's work."

The gates being opened, the whole of these troops took the road to L'Isola della Scala. Now, at two miles from there, there was a village called Servoda, where the knight put the Captain Sucker with the 2000 lansquenets in ambush, promising to lead the enemy under his very nose, and to give him an opportunity of acquiring honour. Bayard and the Baron of Conti, with their troop, marched straight to Isola, without appearing to know who were concealed; they were in a beautiful plain, very open, where they saw at a little distance the Captain Manfroni with some light horse. Bayard sent his standard-bearer, the bastard Du Fay, with some archers, to commence the skirmish, and followed him pretty closely with his soldiers. But he soon saw emerging from Isola the foot-men of Venice, with a troop of soldiers; he affected fright and ordered the trumpet to sound the recall. Thereupon Du Fay, who had his lesson by heart, retired towards the main body and formed with it a single square squadron, which feigning to retire towards Verona, went slowly to the village where was the ambuscade of lansquenets, to whom an archer had been already sent to order them to prepare for battle. The Venetian soldiery, supported by the infantry, charged the French rudely, making a deafening noise with instruments, as though they were sure of victory. The French on their side did not break, and skirmished prudently and with precaution till they had arrived at the village of Sevoda. Then the lansquenets appeared in good order at a bow-shot from the cavalry, and Bayard cried immediately, "Charge!"

The Venetians, already surprised at the sight of the

infantry, whom they did not expect, were very much more astonished at the shock they were obliged to receive from the men-at-arms. Nevertheless, they bore it very well at first, although many of their men were cut down. The lansquenets afterwards fell upon their foot-soldiers, who, having no way of retreat, were cut to pieces; their enemies disdaining to take a single prisoner.

Manfroni, witness of his own defeat, did his duty very well; but seeing no other resource than flight, galloped furiously away towards St. Boniface. He was pursued; but Bayard ordered a retreat, and his whole troop assembled, having made considerable booty, and gained many horses. It also had taken prisoners about sixty men-at-arms, who were led to Verona. The loss of the Venetians was complete. Besides the prisoners already mentioned, twenty-five men-at-arms were left upon the field, and of their 2000 foot-soldiers not one escaped. A triumphant reception was given to the conquerors at Verona. French, Burgundians, and Lansquenets shared the praise, their companions only regretting that they had not been with them.

If this day was glorious for Bayard, and for all those who took part with him, it was still happier by reason of the discovered treason, without which discovery they would all have infallibly perished. However, we must render justice to Bayard's greatness of mind on the two occasions that we are about to speak of. In the first, Manfroni attacks him with 500 men, and prepares an ambuscade of 600 others, Bayard only having 140; in the second, the same use of treason in having him told that he should march with only 300 light horse, and reckoning well that the knight would not have more, he prepares another ambuscade, where he puts 2000 men, to make sure of overwhelming him. The knight, on the contrary, will only take at first 200 soldiers to oppose to 300 of the enemy, and when he knows the treason, instead of revenging himself on Manfroni, and attacking him with superior forces, he contents himself with the same number. This is what he practised during his whole life. He always had a horror of treason and traitors, and we shall see in the course of his history that, after God, he reckoned more on the valour of his troops than on the superiority of their number. When Bayard returned to his quarters, he had the spy brought before him, and said to him, "I have given you my word, and I must keep it. Go to the Venetian camp, and ask the Signor Manfroni if Captain Bayard has done as much as he; and tell him from me that we will see each other again as soon as he likes, at the same price." That said, he had him taken out of the town by two archers. The spy was fool enough to go straight to St. Boniface, but he had hardly arrived there, when Manfroni had him hanged as a traitor, without even hearing a word he had to say.

The winter suspended operations. However, the Venetians, who still held Lignago, and had a good garrison there, often made raids upon that of Verona, which returned the compliment.

At the commencement of this year (1510), that is to say, immediately after Easter, the Duke of Nemours, nephew of the king, went into Italy. He had with him the illustrious Captain Louis d'Ars, of whom we have spoken several times already. They were received in a manner consistent with their rank by the grand-master of Chaumont, governor of Milan, and by all the heads of the army. But no one received more marks of esteem and friendship than Bayard, as well from the prince (who had known him for a long time, and who had been informed of his exploits since they had met) as from Louis d'Ars, his first teacher in the art of fighting. The king sent an addition of 2000 lansquenets and several other captains, under the Lord of Molard, to join the army in Italy.

The grand-master went to lay siege before Lignago, and to cut off his help and provisions, Milaut d'Alègre was sent to Vicenza with 500 men-at-arms, and 4000 or 5000 lansquenets of the brave Prince of Anhalt, who had for his lieutenant the Captain Jacob Emps. The place stood a deal of cannonading a tolerably long time by a numerous artillery, to which was added that of the Duke of Ferrara, where was, amongst others, a culverine of twenty feet long, which the adventurers called *the great devil*. The town was taken at last, and quarter was given to none. Molard and his adventurers did wonders, for they could not wait till the breach should be of a proper size to give the assault. The grand-master placed La Cropte-Daillon there as governor, and with him 100 men-at-arms, of whom he had the charge, under the Marquis of Montferrat, and 1000 foot-soldiers, commanded by the captains Le Hérisson and Jacques Corse, a Neapolitan. During the siege of Lignago, the grand-master heard of the death of his uncle, the Cardinal d'Amboise. He felt this loss so much that he could never be consoled for it. His grief degenerated into a languor, of which he died a short time after, as we shall mention in its place. He was under obligations to this great man for the dignities which he enjoyed, having become successively grand-master, marshal and admiral of France, and governor of the duchy of Milan. This grand prelate, to whom one cannot refuse praise, whenever there is occasion to mention him, had also done much good to all his house, then very numerous, in the church, the court, and the camp. All the historians of his time agree in praising him for the wisdom of his ministry, on the possession of the king's entire confidence, and upon the administration of the finances, which were always abundant, without fresh taxes upon the people, although Louis XII. had almost continual wars to maintain; finally, by his scrupulous disinterestedness, never having wished for more than one benefice. He died Archbishop of Rouen, where his memory is revered to the present day. His death took place, says the historian Bouchet, a short time after the breaking of the treaty of Cambray.

The grand-master of Chaumont, his nephew, notwithstanding his affliction, which he tried to conceal as much as he could, was not less watchful of the interests of the king, his master. Having then provided the guard of Lignago, he went to unite his troops to those of the emperor, to march against the Venetians, and reduce them. Four hundred Spanish and Neapolitan men-at-arms had newly arrived to the assistance of the emperor. They were the finest troops one could see, under the orders of the Duke of Termes.[1] They put them in garrison at Verona to refresh them. The two armies went to camp at a town named Sainte Croix, where they stopped to await the emperor, who was expected; but they waited in vain.

When they left the camp of Sainte Croix to go to Montselles that the Venetians had retaken, a very unfortunate event happened which deserves to be recorded.

---

[1] I have not been able to discover (says M. de Berville) who the Duke of Termes was at the period of which we are writing. There must certainly be an error in the original history.

Near Longara there is a mountain, in which there is a natural cavern, more than a mile in length. The inhabitants of the low country, frightened at the war, had taken refuge there, to the number of 2000 persons, men and women, gentle and simple, with their goods and a quantity of provisions. They had some fire-arms with which to defend the entrance in case of attack, and this entrance was so narrow that only one man at a time could pass through it.

The adventurers, plunderers, of whom the most cowardly are generally foremost, discovered this cave. They wished to enter, but they begged them not to do so, because, said they, those who were within having left their goods in their houses, there was no booty to be obtained. The adventurers thought this advice was only given them to turn them from the project they had formed of penetrating into the cave, and because there was undoubtedly some good capture to make; that is why they determined to force an entrance; but they fired on them from the cavern, and killed two. The others were intimidated by this unexpected event, and dared not undertake a fresh attempt. They despatched some among them to call their comrades, who hastened to the spot, following their custom of being more diligent in the performance of a bad than a good action. When these villains saw that they could not enter by force, they revenged themselves cruelly. They raised a pile of wood, hay, and straw before the mouth of the cave, and set fire to it. In a moment such a stifling smoke arose that the cave was full of it, and the air only entering by this opening, all its occupants were suffocated before the fire had touched one of them.

Among these unhappy victims a number of gentlemen and ladies were found, although dead, as if asleep, and not in the least disfigured. When the smoke had dispersed, the adventurers entered, and made immense booty. Their barbarity horrified the grand-master and all the heads of the army.

But Bayard, who was a sworn enemy to such expeditions, had no rest till he had laid hands on some of these brigands. Two of them fell into his hands, one man with one ear, and the other with none. He made strict inquiries into their mode of life, and found more than was necessary for their deliverance to the provost, who had them hanged before the entrance to the grotto, in presence of Bayard, who wished to be a witness of their punishment.

While the execution was taking place, a kind of phantom issued from the cave, a child of fifteen years, yellowed by smoke, and more dead than alive. He was taken to the knight, who asked him by what miracle he had escaped. The child answered that when he saw the horrible smoke, he fled to the farthest extremity of the cavern, where he had observed the rock broken up above, and that thence he had received a little air. He related also a very deplorable circumstance, which was that some gentlemen and their wives, having seen the preparations for the burning, had wished to go out, at the risk of perishing outside, rather than remain within; but that the peasants shut up with them, and who formed the stronger and the larger number, had prevented them with pikes and other arms, saying, "As we must perish here, you shall also remain."

We have seen that from Sainte Croix the armies turned towards Montselle, that the Venetians had retaken. They had fortified it, and placed there a garrison of 1000 or 1200 men. On the road, Bayard, D'Alègre, and the Lord Mercure, an Albanian captain in the service of the emperor, met a troop of light horse in the service of the republic, whom they called Croates (the troop of Croatia), more Turk than Christian, and noted for plunder. They were coming to see if there was anything to be done, and booty to be gained; but all the good they got by their expedition was to be left nearly all dead on the field or prisoners. Amongst these was a cousin of that Lord Mercure, and his greatest enemy, who had unjustly despoiled him of all his goods in Croatia, their native country. They recognized each other, and the conqueror, remembering all the ill the other had done him, refused to ransom or exchange him, although he remonstrated with him, that as he was a prisoner of war, he ought to enjoy the common right of ransom, and he offered him 6000 ducats and six Turkish horses of admirable beauty.

"We will speak of that at our leisure," said Mercure; "but in good faith, if I were in your power, as you are in mine, what would you do with me?"

"As you press me so much," replied the other, "I declare to you that if you were in my power, as I am in yours, all the gold in the world should not hinder me from cutting you to pieces."

"Truly," said Mercure, "I have no desire to serve you worse."

At that moment he ordered his Albanians to sabre him and his Croates, which was so promptly and so well executed, that there was neither captain nor man who did not receive ten superfluous strokes. Afterwards they cut all their heads off, and bore them in triumph at the end of their pikes, after the manner of the Turks. These Croates wore a singular dress; amongst other things, they had their heads covered with a bonnet made of many sheets of paper pasted together, impenetrable to the sword.

Montselles was besieged and cannonaded for four or five days. It was so well fortified that it would never have been taken without the indiscreet and too frequent sallies of the garrison, which came sometimes within a stone's throw of the fort against the French adventurers, who only wanted to go and see what was going on in the place. One day Captain Molard's men went with a gentleman named the Baron of Montfaucon to skirmish with the men in the castle, who received them gallantly, and repulsed them two or three times with loss, but who finally followed them too far, so that, when they wished to retire, they were so fatigued that they could hardly drag themselves along. When the rest of the garrison saw that all was lost, they retired into a large tower, where they were besieged; and as they would not give themselves up, they set fire to the foot, and the greater part allowed themselves to be burnt rather than to be taken prisoners; others jumped out of the windows, and were received on the point of their pikes. Finally almost all perished. On the French side a gentleman named Camican was killed, and the Baron of Montfaucon was mortally wounded; however, he recovered, but with much difficulty.

CHAPTER X.

HE town of Montselles having been taken, they increased the fortifications, and put a strong garrison there, with the design of going immediately to lay siege to Padua.
While these plans were in progress, they heard that the Pope Julius II. had declared war against the Duke of Ferrara, an ally of the king, to whom this prince had written to obtain help. The king granted it him, and gave orders to the grandmaster, his lieutenant-general, to help the duke. Chaumont, in consequence, sent him a detachment of 4000 men, under the orders of the Lords of Clermont, Montoison, de Fontrailles, du Lude, and Bayard. Added to these were 800 Swiss, newly arrived in the army as adventurers, commanded by a captain of their nation, named Jacob Zemberc. These officers and their troops were received with much joy by the Duke and Duchess of Ferrara and their subjects.

Before speaking of the war between the Pope and the Duke of Ferrara, it will be well in this place to give an account of a check that a party of French received through the treachery of a spy. La Cropte-Daillon was hardly in possession of his government of Lignago, when he fell dangerously ill. He had with him a great number of volunteers, gentlemen. One amongst them was named Guyon de Cantiers, braver and more venturesome than prudent. The Venetians made incursions even to the gates of the town; but the soldiers of the garrison, who only had orders to guard it, dared not go out. Guyon de Cantiers had made acquaintance with the gentlemen of the town of Montagnane, at twelve or fifteen miles from Lignago, who supplied him with spies. One of them often came to see this officer in garrison, and assured him one day that, if he could go out with a small number of horse and foot-soldiers, he would provide him with the means of carrying off the provéditore André Gritti, who often came to Montagnane with two or three hundred light horse. He promised to give him notice of the best day for the occasion, and to show him an ambuscade, where he could place himself in the morning, and whence he could assuredly carry off the provéditore, and immediately afterwards take the town, where there was plenty of plunder to be had. Cantiers, who was no less eager to signalize himself by an exploit than to take possession of this booty, promised to act as the spy directed, and charged him to warn him of the exact time.

This traitor, having returned to Montagnane, told the commander of his agreement with Cantiers, and promised to give him up a party from the garrison of Lignago, and to give him the power of retaking the place even, which was of consequence to the Venetian senate. The commander thought of the project, and by an express informed the provéditore of it, who immediately sent 300 men-at-arms, 800 light horse, and 2000 foot-soldiers.

The very same day the spy returned to Cantiers, who

was charmed to see him, and asked him what news he brought. "Very good for you, if you will profit by it," he answered in a confident tone. "The provéditore arrives this evening in our town with only 100 horse. If you will be in the country to-morrow before day, I will give him up to you." Cantiers, transported with joy, ran to announce this news to his companions, amongst others to a gentleman who was their standard-bearer, named young Malherbe. Every one wished to take part in the expedition; but to do so the permission of the commander, La Cropte-Daillon, was necessary, who, being still ill, kept his room. Cantiers and Malherbe went to ask him, and related the enterprise as the most glorious and advantageous in the world. La Cropte was too wise to profit by their advice at first. "You know," said he, "that the place has been confided to me alone on my life and honour, to keep it. If any misfortune happened to you, I should be a dishonoured man, and I should die of grief, so I cannot allow you to adopt this plan." They insisted more strongly than before, assuring him that their spy was a safe man; finally, they said so much to him that rather by force or importunity than of his own good-will he gave them leave.

The provéditore had sent as ambuscade, at two or three miles round Montagnane, 200 men-at-arms and 1000 foot-soldiers, with orders to let pass all that went out from Lignago, and to cut off the passage from behind, which plan was only too well carried out for the unfortunate Cantiers and his companions.

These, who would have taken permission themselves if their commander had refused it, gave notice to their troop, of the hour when it would be necessary to be on horseback, to the number of fifty men-at-arms, under the orders of Malherbe, and 300 foot-soldiers, led by Cantiers, and they set out from Lignago just before two o'clock, guided by their faithless spy, who led them to butchery.

They followed the high road from Lignago to Montagnane, the foot-soldiers before, and the cavalry forming the wing, passed without challenge a little village, where the first ambuscade was, and advanced to within a mile of the town. There the spy left them, to go, as he said, to see what was going on at Montagnane. They let him go; but they might better have killed him, for he went straight to the provéditore, and said to him, "I have brought you the best part of the garrison of Lignago with the rope round their necks, and, if you like, not one of them can escape you. They are at about a mile from here, and less than that from the ambuscade. Gritti was soon on horseback with all his men, and sent 200 horse forward to skirmish. The French were full of joy, thinking that the provéditore was in this first party, and that they were going to capture him. They charged the company vigorously, but the men turned and fled towards the chief ambuscade. Then the great secret was explained, and the French, greatly astonished, returned to their foot-soldiers, and said to them, "We are lost; they are more than 3000; we must try to save ourselves." The Venetians followed closely on their heels crying, "Marco, slaughter!"

The French, seeing the danger, put their foot-soldiers in front, and the cavalry behind, to support them, and in this manner retreated, without loss, to the village where the first Venetian ambuscade was. These showed themselves immediately at the sound of the trumpet, in the order that they were, and shut out the road to

Lignago from the French, who found themselves surrounded by a number ten times as large as their own. However, they defended themselves like lions, and occupied this great number more than four hours without being broken. Then Gritti sent his cross-bowmen to attack the foot-soldiers on the flank, which soon scattered them, but did not hinder them from retiring to within four miles from their place. Finally attacked on all sides, their men-at-arms dismounted, the greater part of their horses slain, and only one to ten of their adversaries, they were obliged to yield, and in such a manner, that out of three hundred not one was left. Cantiers, their captain, seeing that all was lost, threw himself upon the enemy, and slew six with his own hand before he perished himself. Malherbe continued an hour longer with his men-at-arms, and was at last made prisoner with twenty-five of his men; all the rest were slain. Not one man remained to carry the news to Lignago.

The provéditore Gritti, seeing that his victory was so complete, thought of a stratagem to surprise Lignago. He had all the dead Frenchmen stripped, and their dress put upon as many of his own soldiers, both foot and horse. Then he gave them 120 of his men to lead as prisoners, with three falconers that the French had brought, and he ordered them to go to the town, and to cry on arriving, " France! France! victory! victory!" " Those in the town," said he, " will think their own men have arrived victorious; and to deceive them better, carry their standards with some of ours, as if you had gained them. They will certainly open the gate to you, and you can seize it. I shall march at a bowshot from you, and join you at the first sound of the trumpet. If you play your parts well, Lignago will be ours in the day, and you know of what importance it is to the Republic."

This order was perfectly executed. The Venetians approached the place to the sound of trumpets and clarions, and began crying, "Victory!" La Cropte had a lieutenant named Bernard de Villars, a man of quality, an old and experienced soldier, who, seeing this triumphant troop approach, went up to the donjon of the gate to reconnoitre it. He suspected the marching and the countenances of both the foot and horse soldiers. "These are the dresses and horses of our men," said he; "but they are not mounted in the French fashion; they do not manage their horses as we do. My heart tells me that our men have met with some misfortune, and that this is only a stratagem." Under this idea he sent a man to have the drawbridge lowered and raised again. "If these are our men," said he, "you will recognize them; if not, save yourselves behind the barrier. I have two pieces of loaded cannon, with which I shall receive them." The soldier executed the order. He went out of the place to reconnoitre the troop, and cried, "Who goes there? Where is Captain Malherbe?" None answered; but the enemy, thinking that the bridge would be down, spurred their horses. The soldier gained the barrier in haste; then they discharged the two pieces of cannon, which stopped the astonished troop, and made them turn back. Thus the place was saved; but the day had been only too unfortunate.

When Daillon learnt this news he thought he should have died of grief. The king was near bringing him to trial; but Marshal Trivulce appeased him. He was then at the court to stand godfather to Madame Renée, second daughter of the king, and as he knew Daillon to be a good officer, he justified him, and obtained his pardon.

But we must resume the account of the war declared against the Duke of Ferrara by the pope, which we interrupted to relate this occurrence.

CHAPTER XI.

N 1511, Julius II, claiming the Duchy of Ferrara as a possession of the Holy See, and wishing to reunite it, raised an army in the Bologna, and to carry it through this duchy he took it to a town named Santo Felice, between Concordia and La Mirandola. The duke on his side, and the French whom he had with him, had come to lodge at twelve miles from Ferrara, between the two branches of the Po, at a place called the Ospitaletto, and they made a bridge of boats, upon which they put a strong guard, and by this bridge they made frequent skirmishes.

When the pope had arrived at Santo Felice, he sent a haughty message to the Countess of La Mirandola, desiring her to return the town to him, because it was necessary for his expedition to Ferrara. This lady, who was a natural daughter of Marshal Trivulce, of whom we have just spoken, was the widow of Louis-Marie Picot.[1] Like her father's, her heart was entirely French; and as she had been informed that the Duke of Ferrara

---

[1] The Loyal Servant says "natural daughter to the Lord John James of Trivulce, and then a widow."

was an ally of France, and that the king sent aid to him, she would not, at the risk of her life, have given up her town to the pope. She had with her at the time her cousin-german, the Count Alexander Trivulce, with whom she planned the answer that she should return to the holy father's message. She told the deputy to return, and tell his master that the countess would not give up her town at any price whatever; that God had made her lady and mistress of it, and she knew how to guard it against whoever wished to wrest it from her.

The pope, irritated to the last degree by this answer, swore by St. Peter and St. Paul that he would make himself master of it by fair or foul means, and he ordered his nephew, and captain-general of his army, the Duke of Urbino, to prepare himself at once to besiege it the next day. The Count Alexander, who had expected this, sent in all haste to acquaint the Duke of Ferrara and the French generals at La Mirandola with what had happened. He told them that, not having enough soldiers to defend the town, he begged them to send them a hundred brave men and two chief artillerymen. The keeping of La Mirandola interested the Duke of Ferrara[2] so much that he immediately sent the required help.

With the 100 men and the two artillerists set out as volunteers two French gentlemen, the Lords of Mont-

---

[2] This duke was named Alphonse I, son of Hercules I. He was a great captain, wise and vigilant in war, and a good politician. He was a man learned in the arts and sciences, and he was especially noted for his skill in engineering and mathematics, even to the extent of the casting of artillery, and the construction of gun carriages.

chenu[3] and of Chantemerle; the first a native of Dauphiny, nephew of the illustrious Montoison, and the other from Beausse, a nephew of the Lord of Lude. On their leaving, Bayard exhorted them to signalize themselves, and to get themselves a name. "The place you are going to," said he, " is well fortified and strong, and you are going to fight in the service of a lady; you ought to make yourselves worthy of her good graces; and if the place is besieged you will have the honour of keeping it for her."

After other encouraging words, he escorted his company on horseback to the town, and saw them enter it. They were received by the lady and the count with all possible joy and honours. Three days after, the place was besieged. The artillery was planted on the borders of the ditch, and fired without intermission; while that of the town answered in like manner, and the besieged did not appear afraid of the pope's forces.

Bayard, who had spies everywhere, and was well served because he paid well, knew every day exactly what was passing at Santo Felice in the pope's camp. One of these spies, having informed him that the pope intended to set out shortly to come and command the siege of La Mirandola in person, he sent him back to find out the precise time at which he would start. The spy returned, and told him that it would be on the morning of the next day.

The good knight, without fail, without fear, and without reproach, charmed at this news, determined to

---

[3] Marin de Montchenu, the favourite of Francis I, and afterwards first steward of his household. He followed this prince (not because he was a prisoner, but simply on account of his attachment) in his captivity at Madrid, after the fatal battle of Pavia.

make a bold stroke, and carry off the pope and all his court.

He went to the Duke of Ferrara's, where he found the Lord of Montoison. "I am informed," he told them, "that to-morrow the pope leaves his camp at Santo Felice, to go to that of La Mirandola, six miles distant. I have a plan that I have come to propose to you, and if you agree to it, it will be talked of a hundred years hence; it is this: At two miles from Santo Felice I know of two or three large palaces, abandoned on account of the war. With 100 men-at-arms of my choice, I will place myself in ambush in one of these palaces, and to-morrow morning, when the pope leaves, carry him off. I know that he will only be escorted by some cardinals, some bishops and prothonotaries, with 100 men of his guard; so before the alarm shall have reached his camp, I will bring him here to you. But to help me, in case of accident, it will be necessary, my lord," he said, turning to the duke, "that you and the Lord of Montoison should cross the bridge at break of day with the rest of the soldiery, and that you should advance to four or five miles from here." This plan was approved of; there was nothing now but to put it in execution, which was not delayed a moment: for Bayard, having taken his 100 picked men, put them in battle order, as if they were marching to an action, and in this manner they travelled all night, having the spy for a guide. He had the good fortune to be lodged in one of the palaces before day, without having been met or discovered by man or woman.

CHAPTER XII.

AT daybreak the pope got into a litter, and took the road to his camp at La Mirandola. His prothonotaries, secretaries, and other household officers had set out before him to prepare his apartments. When Bayard saw this cortège he fell upon it without loss of time, but they drew bridle, and ran as fast as all their legs could carry them, to take the alarm to Santo Felice. That was not what saved the pope, however; fortunately for him, as soon as he had entered his litter, and before he was a hundred steps from Santo Felice, it snowed so heavily that the Cardinal of Pavia, (Felix Alidosi), his prime minister, represented to him that the severity of the weather would not allow of the journey, and advised him to return, to which the pope consented.

As bad luck would have it, the fugitives arrived disconcerted and out of breath just as the pope reached the castle, and the good knight Bayard the town; for the latter, only desiring one object, did not stop to amuse himself with taking other prisoners.

The pope was so frightened at their cries that he jumped out of his litter without assistance, and himself helped to raise the bridge. There was no time to lose, for in an instant later he would have been caught up and taken prisoner.

However mortified Bayard might be at this mishap, he had no other plan but to return. He knew, however, that the castle was worth nothing, and that he should have it in a quarter of an hour; but having no artillery, and no time to send for it, he was fearful that the alarm taken to the camp of La Mirandola should result in assistance to the pope, help that he did not think it necessary to wait for. So he took the road to Ferrara with as many prisoners as he chose, amongst which were two bishops, and a great number of baggage mules, which last his soldiers had the benefit of. Bayard was inconsolable at the failure of this well-laid plan. The Dukes of Ferrara and Montoison, whom he found at the appointed meeting-place with their escort, were not less grieved when he gave them his account of it. However, they showed him that the evil was without remedy; that his plan was admirable, and that chance alone had hindered its success. They led him back with them to the camp, and on the way they sent back several of their prisoners on foot, and afterwards liberated the two bishops for a moderate ransom.

The pope was so much frightened at the danger he had run, that he shook as if he had the ague for twenty-four hours, and the following night he sent a special messenger to fetch his nephew the Duke of Urbino, who joined him with 400 men-at-arms to conduct him to the camp at La Mirandola. When he was there he carried on the siege so vigorously that the place was forced to give up. The same luck which had left him his liberty rendered him master of it, for during the siege the snow fell for six successive days and nights, and so abundantly that it lay on the ground within the camp to the height of a man. To the snow succeeded such a severe frost, that the moats of La Mirandola were two feet thick in ice, and a cannon with its carriage, which fell upon it, could not break it.

The pope's artillery had already made two wide breaches, so that the countess and the Count Alexander, having no hope of help, were obliged to capitulate. They knew that the grand master of Chaumont was at Reggio with the rest of the French army fortifying that place, not doubting that after the reduction of La Mirandola the pope might attack it with all his forces, which had become considerable by the union of the Spanish and Venetian troops with it. They asked by the capitulation that the town having surrendered to the pope, he should promise that the garrison and inhabitants should have their lives saved, but he wished all to give themselves up at discretion. However the Duke of Urbino was the mediator, and treated to the satisfaction of both parties. The pope would not have been so merciful had it not been for the friendship he felt for his nephew, whose heart was entirely in favour of the French, and who remembered with gratitude the kindness that the reigning king, whose page he had been, had shown to him. The holy father did not condescend to enter La Mirandola by the gate; he had a bridge made on the moat, and entered there by the breach.

The news of this taking grieved the Duke of Ferrara and all the French generals. This prince, little doubting that he should be incessantly besieged in his capital, broke the bridge, and shut himself up in it with all his troops, resolved to defend himself to the last extremity. In fact Julius was no sooner quiet in La Mirandola than he assembled a council of war, at which the Duke of Urbino and all the cavalry and infantry officers of the army assisted, and declared before them all that, without losing a moment, he would lay siege to Ferrara. He asked them their advice as to the manner of this expedition, taking into consideration that the place was strong in itself, and that it was provided with good troops and numerous artillery. He added that the best means of reducing it would be to cut off the provisions, and starve it out, which would not be difficult, as he was master of the upper passage of the Po, provided the Venetians would guard the lower. Every one said what he liked for or against this plan; when the turn of one of the captains of the republic, named Giovanni Forti, came, he spoke to the pope, and said to him:—

"Very Holy Father, following the plan of your holiness, and the opinions of all those who have spoken, it should appear very easy to starve Ferrara by guarding the upper and lower passages of the Po; but I know the country well enough to be certain that the place could obtain sufficient subsistence from Argenta,—we could, however, cut off even this resource; on the other side there is a country that they call the Polesine of St. George, so rich that it alone would nourish the town for one year. Now, it will be difficult to break off communication with it, if your holiness does not get rid of a little town at twenty miles from Ferrara, named La Bastia, which, once taken, I warrant the place starved out in less than two months, considering the number of people shut up in it."

The captain had hardly finished speaking, when the pope cried out that they must have La Bastia, and that they should have no rest until the place was theirs; and he instantly gave the commission to two Spanish captains, who were each to lead 100 men-at-arms, and to the Captain Forti with 500 horses and from 5000 to 6000 foot-soldiers. He gave them besides six pieces of heavy artillery.

All this large train of artillery set out in haste, arrived before the place without hindrance, and surprised the governor, who did not expect to be besieged, more especially by such a formidable army. However, he resolved to defend himself well—as well as he could with such a feeble garrison as his, and he sent a special messenger to his master, to inform him of the extremity in which he found himself. The pope's men did not lose a moment. As soon as they had arrived, they planted their artillery, and began making a breach.

CHAPTER XIII.

HE courier that the governor had at first sent secretly to the duke marched with such diligence that he was at Ferrara in six hours. Bayard met him at the gate by which he entered, and had him brought forward to know who he was, whence he came, and what his business at Ferrara was.

This man gave him a faithful account of his commission, of the arrival of from 7000 to 8000 men before La Bastia, and finished up by saying that the governor sent word to the duke that if he were not speedily assisted, he could not hold out twenty-four hours.

"What!" cried Bayard, "is the place so bad as that?"

"No, my lord," replied the messenger, "it is one of the best places in Italy, but there are only twenty-five men within, who are not in a state to resist, especially if their enemies give the assault."

Upon that Bayard led him to the duke, whom he found on horseback in the market-place, in company with Montoison.

This latter, believing that the knight had a spy, cried out to him from a distance, "My companion, you would sooner die than pass a day without capturing some of the enemy. How much is this prisoner going to pay for his ransom?"

"He is not an enemy," said Bayard, "he brings strange news for my lord."

The messenger gave the duke the letters of the governor of La Bastia, who immediately began reading them. At every word he changed colour; they saw him grow red and white by turns.

When he had finished reading the letter, he said, with a sorrowful air, "If I lose La Bastia, I may also abandon Ferrara, and I do not see any means of giving help there in the time that my commander points out; for he asks it for to-morrow, and that is absolutely impossible, taking into consideration that it is twenty miles from here to La Bastia, and more than that, there is a defile half a mile long, where only one man can pass at a time, and if my enemies knew of another pass which is on the road, with twenty men they could stop 10,000; but I do not think they know of it."

Bayard, seeing the prince in consternation, and with so much reason for it, said to him, "My lord, for great evils we must have great remedies. When a little thing is in hand, we may leave it to chance; but when ruin is before us, we ought to employ our most strenuous efforts to ward it off. Your enemies believe themselves in safety before La Bastia, because they imagine that the pope's army, which is not far from here, will hinder our going to pay them a visit. An idea occurs to me of a plan, which I do not think it will be difficult to execute, and which, if it succeeded, would do us great honour. You have in this town 4000 or 5000 good troops, experienced soldiers. Take 2000 of them, with the 800 Swiss of the Captain Zemberc, and make them embark to-night. You are still master of the Po as far as Argenta. Order them to go and await us at the passage of which you have just spoken, and to take it from them, if they are arrived before us. The gendarmerie will march all night by land, with good guides, and will be there to-morrow at sunrise, and join us. The enemy will never suspect our march. You say that from this passage to La Bastia is only three miles; that being so, without giving them time to range themselves in battle order, we will fall upon them. I have an idea that we shall succeed."

All the gold in the world would not have been so acceptable to the duke, as the advice Bayard had just given him.

"My lord Bayard," he cried, transported with joy, "you find nothing difficult, and I do not doubt that if all the French lords who are here will help us, we shall destroy the pope's army," and, added he, taking his hat off, "I beg them to do so with all my heart."

"There is no necessity for that," replied the brave Montoison. "Order, and you shall be obeyed, for the king, our master, told us so to do. The lords of Lude and Fontrailles say the same, and they are not men to retract."

At the same time they sent for the captains of the foot-soldiers, who were in the same mind, and charmed with the idea of the expedition.

The duke secretly prepared a number of boats, and made all his foot-soldiers embark in them that evening, with good and skilful sailors. The cavalry set out at the approach of night, the duke at their head, with good guides, who led them so well that, notwithstanding the bad weather, half an hour before daybreak they arrived without any obstacle or mishap at the passage where they were to meet the others. At break of day the boats with the foot-soldiers arrived also. When all were assembled, they marched noiselessly towards the difficult passage, which was a little bridge, so narrow that only one knight could pass at a time, and it was over a very deep torrent between the Po and La Bastia. They were an hour crossing, so that it was quite light when they had all arrived on the other side. This circumstance lessened their chances of success in the duke's opinion, and besides that, they did not hear the cannon, which made them think the place had surrendered. But while they were talking with the French captains, they heard three cannons fire at once, which gave them inexpressible pleasure.

They were then at a mile from the hostile army, and Bayard, addressing himself to the duke, said, " My lord, I have heard say that it is not wise to count your enemy for nothing. We are very near ours, and if they had the least knowledge of our march, they would give us a great deal of trouble, for they are three to our one. They have artillery, and we have none. Besides, the pope has sent here the pick of his troops, so we must do the best we possibly can to surprise them. My advice is, that the bastard Du Fay, my standard-bearer, a man learned in skirmishes, should go and give them the alarm on the side whence they have come, with only fifteen or twenty horse, and the Captain Pierrepont, with 100 men-at-arms, shall follow him at a bowshot's length to sustain him, and at a like distance the Captain Zemberc shall march with his Swiss. You, my lord, at our head with the Lord of Montoison, and all the French captains that are here, will march straight to the siege, and I will go a little in advance to give the first alarm. If Du Fay attacks before us, and the enemy turns to his side, we will put them between him and us. If, on the other hand, we attack before him, Pierrepont and the Swiss will act as we should have done under the same circumstances. By that means they will be astonished, and will think our number three times as large as it is; and our trumpets must make as much noise as they possibly can."

This arrangement having been approved of by every one, they agreed to follow the advice; and they set out on their march from opposite points. The prince's detachment arrived at a cannon-shot from the place, and neither party was yet discovered.

Du Fay commenced by giving a loud alarm from his side, which surprised all the enemy's camp greatly. They immediately put themselves under arms, and mounted their horses to go straight to him, while their foot-soldiers ranged themselves in battle order; but, fortunately for the Duke of Ferrara, they did not give them the time. Those who repulsed Du Fay had hardly taken 200 steps when Pierrepont attacked them from the side, and broke them. The Swiss immediately fell upon the foot-soldiers, who were from 5000 to 6000 in number. They had not much success at first, and would have been undoubtedly forced to yield to numbers, had it not been for the cavalry, which sustained them, and took this infantry on the flank. Then the duke, at the head of the French men-at-arms, commanded by Montoison, Du Lude, Fontrailles, and Bayard, and with 200 foot-soldiers attacked the enemy in the rear, and completely defeated them. While these deeds were being done, Fontrailles and Bayard perceived a body of from 300 to 400 knights, who tried to rally. They called their men together promptly, who, without giving their enemies time to recognize them, charged them crying, "France! France! duke! duke!" and upset the greater part of them. The rest of their army sustained the shock for nearly an hour, notwithstanding the slaughter, but finally their defeat was so complete that very few escaped. Five thousand foot-soldiers and more than sixty men-at-arms, all the baggage, all the artillery, and more than three hundred horses, remained to the conquerors, with so much plunder that it was quite embarrassing.

CHAPTER XIV.

THIS victory of La Bastia was the salvation of the Duke of Ferrara, and the French, who, under other circumstances, had been lost. They all returned to Ferrara glorious and triumphant, and were received there with shouting and acclamation by the people. The duchess especially gave them the reception due to their success, and during their stay regaled them with continual festivals and amusements. We have spoken of the virtues and talents of the duke. The duchess, his wife, was not less worthy of praise. She was Anne Sforza, daughter of Galéas Marie, Duke of Milan, and Bonne of Savoy, daughter of the Duke Louis. Nature had bestowed upon her more gifts and graces than upon any other woman of her age. She spoke and composed equally well in Italian, French, Latin, and Greek, and contributed not a little to the glory of her husband and his house. They had one son, Hercules II, Duke of Ferrara, who married Madame Renée, second daughter of the king.

We are compelled to interrupt the course of our narrative for a short time to do homage to the rare talents of our hero. The Duke of Ferrara owed to him the safety of his estates. The French army was no less under an obligation to him, for it would undoubtedly have been lost if the pope had succeeded in his plans, in league as he was with the Spanish and the Venetians. What wonderful presence of mind at the news of the siege of La Bastia! what coolness in seeking for a remedy! what promptitude in finding it! what wisdom in its development! finally, what a display of sagacity and generalship in its execution! But it is impossible sufficiently to praise Bayard for the part he performed on this memorable occasion. He had never seen La Bastia nor its environs, nor the local situation of the Po; but he had a perfect knowledge of it nevertheless. Without this knowledge he could never have conceived and carried into execution a plot so complicated, and upon the success of which depended the saving of the duke and of his estates, and that of the army of the king himself.

A few months after the great event just recorded, Philibert de Clermont, Lord of Montoison, died at Ferrara, of a fever, which carried him off in a few days. He was lieutenant-general of the French army in Italy, and one of the greatest captains of his age. He distinguished himself greatly in Picardy, Bretagne, Lombardy, and the kingdom of Naples. He had gained great advantages over the Swiss, particularly at the Lake of Como. He was praised amongst other qualities for the singular precision he showed in deciding the number of a hostile army, however far it might be from him. The king was full of regret at his death. He looked upon him as the first of his captains, and feared that his death would occasion a revolt in the duchy of Milan. He was much regretted by the Duke and Duchess of Ferrara, and by all the officers, both French and Italian; but Bayard wept for him, his particular friend and his countryman.[1]

If the deliverance of La Bastia was glorious happiness for the French, it was equally intolerable misery to the pope, who was furious when he received news of it. He swore to be avenged, and wished to go immediately and lay siege to Ferrara; but his generals tried by all means in their power to turn him from his intention. His nephew, the Duke of Urbino, especially was loud in dispraise of such a proceeding, as he wished to see his uncle reconciled to the king of France. They represented to him that the place was strong in itself, well furnished with artillery, and full of good officers, of whom the invincible Bayard was one; that he would not only lose his men, but have great difficulty in obtaining ammunition and provisions.

Julius, obliged to give up the idea of taking the place by force, plotted to have it by surprise, making use of spies upon whom he thought he could rely, and by whose means he hoped to get one of the gates opened secretly in the night.

He sent spies, therefore, charged to draw the sentinels from their duty; but the duke and the knight were so wary that they arrested six or seven of these spies, who

---

[1] They were both from the same canton, in the province of Dauphiny. Montoison was captain of fifty men-at-arms, and one of the most illustrious warriors of his heroic age. He was the originator of the device that descended to his posterity, *à la recousse, Montoison*, "to the rescue, Montoison," on the occasion of the battle of Fornova, when Charles VIII, seeing a wing of his army tottering, and ready to break, cried *To the rescue, Montoison!* Montoison, who was in command of the rear-guard, went at once, and charged the enemy so vigorously that he decided the gain of the battle. This brave man belonged to a cadet branch of the house of Clermont Tonnerre.

were hanged. However, the Duke of Ferrara entertained suspicions (perhaps wrongfully) of some of the gentlemen of the town, amongst others of the Count Borse of the house of Calcagnini, with whom Bayard had once lodged, and at whose detention he was much grieved; but he felt that in the uncertain state of affairs it would not be prudent to interfere.

The pope's plan of taking Ferrara by treason not being more satisfactory than his wish to besiege it, he imagined a third scheme, which was truly horrible. It was his intention to endeavour to enlist the Duke of Ferrara on his side against the French, who had always been the duke's best friends and most valuable allies. Julius had in his service a gentleman of Lodi, in the Duchy of Milan, named Augustin Guerlo, a celebrated intriguer, and a man always more ready to do a treasonable than a good action. The pope sent for him one day, and charged him to go secretly to the Duke of Ferrara, and tell him that if he would ally himself with him, for the purpose of utterly destroying the French, he would give one of his nieces to his eldest son in marriage, with the title of Gonfalonier and Captain-general of the church, and bind to him for ever the estates and possessions which had been the causes of quarrels between them. "It will be only necessary," Julius continued, "for him to give the French their leave, and tell them that he has no further occasion for their services, and as they must pass my territory on their return, my intention is, not to let one escape me."

Guerlo found the commission very much to his taste, and undertook it immediately, promising the pope to acquit himself to his satisfaction. He went to Ferrara. and addressed himself at once to the Duke, who listened to him calmly, and without showing any of the intense horror he felt at such a dastardly proposal; on the contrary, he pretended to the messenger that he would willingly comply with the pope's wishes, though nothing was further from his intention, and he would have preferred losing all his estates, and death even, to acting in a manner so treacherous and ungrateful, and unworthy of himself. However, he received the messenger well, and had him apparently well treated; but he ordered him to be taken to a room, of which he shut the door, and took away the key, and, accompanied by only one gentleman, proceeded at once to Bayard's lodgings.

The tale of the evil design of Julius made the good knight shudder, as well it might; in fact, the plot appeared to him so thoroughly detestable that he hesitated to believe it at first. But the duke offered to convince him, if he would return to his palace with him, by placing him in a cabinet, whence he could hear Guerlo repeat the pope's commission word for word, assuring him that, after the tokens the envoy had given him, he could not doubt that he was really sent by the pope; "but," added he, "when I heard it I shuddered with horror as you do. I know the obligations my ancestors were under to the kings of France, and myself more than all to the reigning king, and rather than repay their services by such vile treason, I would consent to be bound to four horses, and torn limb from limb."

Bayard told him that he had no reason to justify himself, that he knew his greatness of mind too well to fear that any surprise could happen to the French, at least with his consent, and that he felt himself as safe in Ferrara as at Paris.

Then the duke proposed to act somewhat as the pope had done, and to repay his intended good turn by one somewhat similar, and, without explaining what he meant, he returned to the palace, where he conversed with Guerlo some time without coming to the point. At last he said, "I fear the holy father's scheme is not practicable for two reasons. In the first place, how can he expect me to trust him, after he has told me a hundred times that I am the man he hates the most in the world, and that if he had me in his power he would murder me; and I know besides that he has no other motive than to obtain possession of my town and estates. In the second place, how can I have the assurance to declare to the Lord Bayard and the other French captains that their aid is useless, and that they must leave? They are twice as strong as I am here; they will take time to inform the king or his lieutenant-general, the grandmaster of Chaumont; and if while waiting their orders, they hear of my understanding with the pope, they will have a right to treat me as a man without faith, and perhaps an enemy, or at least they will leave me, and I shall find myself exposed on all sides. But, Signor Guerlo, you know the pope is a terrible, furious, and vindictive man. He has spoken one thing to you, and possibly thinks another, and he is quite capable of paying you treacherously on the first day of your services. Besides, he is mortal, and when he is dead what reward will you have from his successors? Are you not aware that in that court gratitude for services does not pass from one pope to another? You know that I am in a position to do you good, and I give you my word that I will do it so generously that you shall be at ease for the rest of your life, if you will help me to defeat my enemy."

Guerlo was too low-minded and interested to refuse such propositions. He assured the prince that for a long time he had resolved to leave the pope's service for his, if he agreed to it; that no one was more able than he to do what he wished, being day and night with the pope, serving him at table, and being so much in his confidence that they talked together alone of the most secret matters."

" So, my lord," he added, "if you will make it worth my while, he shall not be alive in eight days from this. I ask for no reward till after his death; but I must have your word that when that takes place I shall be well remembered."

The duke, who had already given him his word, confirmed it on his honour, and they agreed that Guerlo should receive 2000 ducats down, and 500 ducats a year.

The treaty concluded, the duke left the messenger to inform Bayard of what had happened. He found him on the ramparts, and, having drawn him aside, said to him, " You know that traitors and deceivers often fall into their own traps. You and I, and all the French, shall soon be avenged on our enemy. I have gained over the pope's commissioner, and I have his word that in eight days his master shall be a dead man."

" How can that be," cried Bayard, " does this man so enter into the secrets of Providence that he can predict the precise time of life or death ?"

" Do not disturb yourself," the duke replied, " I am very certain of what I have just said."

Bayard's heart was too pure to suspect the truth; but, having finally learnt that Guerlo was to poison the pope, he trembled, and manifested his great surprise at the duke, wondered how such a plot could have originated with so great a prince, and said that if he could think such a thing possible, he would warn the pope of it that very day.

The duke justified himself by saying with what horrible treason the pope had intended to act towards them, and reminded Bayard how many of his spies they had arrested and hanged.

"No matter," said Bayard, "I can never consent to his perishing in that manner."

The duke, on the contrary, wished that all his enemies might be served the same; "but," he added, "as you oppose it, it shall not be, but if God himself do not smite him, and that soon, you and I will have plenty of time to repent our mercy."

"I hope not," replied Bayard, "and if you will give up to me the man who wishes to commit this masterpiece of villany, I will have him hanged in less than an hour."

The duke, who had pledged his word to Guerlo that his person should be safe, kept his promise, and sent him away. But the miserable wretch had not long to wait for the reward that he merited, having been hanged some time after at Brescia for another crime. Thus Bayard, who had checked the plots of the pope against the duke, and the schemes of the duke against the pope, saved the life of the one and the honour and estates of the other.

CHAPTER XV.

JULIUS remained some time longer at La Mirandola, then put his troops in their quarters, and returned to Rome. About this time the Duke of Urbino, the pope's nephew, had a quarrel with the Cardinal of Pavia, the prime minister, and killed him. How the quarrel arose is not exactly known, but it was imagined that the cardinal had accused the young duke of favouring the French, and informing them daily of his uncle's plans. The pope was irritated at the death of his favourite, but he did nothing to avenge it. We know well enough the privileges belonging to the position of nephew to the pope.

In the following year (1512) Trivulce, who had become Marshal of France, and who was in command of the French army in Lombardy, re-took La Mirandola, and gave it back to the countess. Afterwards he drove the pope's army to Bologna, where he entirely destroyed it, and thought to make the pontiff himself prisoner. This victory was remarkable, inasmuch as no blood was shed. All was taken—men, artillery, tents, and baggage. There were some of the French who took five or six prisoners single-handed—one of them named La Baume, who had a wooden leg, led three bound together. Bayard acquired so much glory on this extraordinary day, that Marshal Trivulce did not hesitate to say on the same evening, in presence of all the officers of the army, that it was to him, after God, that they owed the victory.

Before this great victory much had been taking place in Italy; but as the events have nothing to do with our hero, we suppress them. We ought not, however, to omit that the emperor, having some places in Friuli that the Venetians kept from him, asked help from France to recover them. The king sent him 1200 men-at-arms and 800 foot-soldiers, commanded by Chabannes, who did not forget to engage his good friend Bayard to accompany him. This body met the emperor's army (under the orders of George of Stein, a German lord) at Verona. Thence it marched straight to Trevisa, whence, not having had great success, it penetrated into Friuli.

Bayard at that time was in command of 100 men-at-arms, whom the king had recently given to the Duke of Lorraine, with the express condition that the knight should head them. With this troop, accompanied by the brave Fontrailles and his men, and some few Germans, they presented themselves before Gradisca and Goritz, soon made themselves masters of them, and gave them up to the emperor's soldiers; but, disgusted by the slowness of the Germans, they rejoined Chabannes, who, for the same reason, was still where they had left him. In this expedition they lost an excellent officer, the Lord of Lorges (of the house of Montgomery), who was killed before Trevisa, and who commanded 1000 foot-soldiers. Misery followed, and more than 4000 men, French as well as Grisons, died for want of provisions. This state of things determined

Chabannes to return, notwithstanding the opposition of the emperor's soldiers, with whom he had high words on this subject.

After Mirandola had been retaken, and Ferrara assisted as we have seen, the Duke of Nemours, with the French officers, went to see the Duke and Duchess of Ferrara in their Capital, and had a reception worthy of a prince who was the nephew of a king, and of the great service that the French had rendered them. Amongst many sights, there was one of which we shall give an account, less to serve as a model than to show to what excess of fury they carried what they called bravery, or a point of honour, in those days. It appears incredible that princes and lords, noted for their birth, their virtues, their piety even, should lend themselves to combats which are revolting to nature and reason, as if they were legitimate and reasonable acts, some fighting, others seconding them, others judging them, and again others looking on. We have seen Bayard himself, the wisest and most virtuous man of his age, doing the same thing. But the most astonishing part is to see the combatants preparing themselves by prayer to fight, and the conqueror giving thanks to God for having killed his man.

Two Spanish gentlemen, the one the Lord of St. Croix, the other Azevedo, made prisoners at Bologna, had quarrelled. Azevedo accused St. Croix of having wished to assassinate him treasonably. St. Croix had given him the lie, and had offered to satisfy him by mortal combat. Azevedo charged the Baron of Bearn to obtain permission to fight from the Duke of Nemours, which was granted. He then sent for St. Croix, who accepted the challenge immediately. The field was prepared before the Duke of Ferrara's palace. The second

K

day the champions appeared. St. Croix, accompanied by 100 knights, amongst others by Dom Pedro d'Acugna, his second, knight of Rhodes, and grand prior of Messina, and other lords. Azevedo was attended by the same number, and his second, Frederick of Gonzagues, Count of Bossola. As soon as Azevedo had entered the lists, armed with all possible weapons for fighting either on horseback or on foot, the grand prior of Messina advanced towards him, and presented him with two very sharp swords and two poniards, from which he was to choose,[1] St. Croix not intending to have any other kind of arms. After their seconds had felt them to satisfy themselves that they had no coats of mail or other defence under their clothes, they fell on their knees, and said their prayers, and every one left the field but the two seconds and Bayard, whom the Duke of Ferrara had appointed umpire, not only to honour him, but because he knew most about such fights. The herald having sounded to impose silence, the two adversaries marched proudly towards each other, and commenced fighting. Their strokes fell so thick and fast that one did not wait for the other, and both had need to be watchful and careful of their footing. After several strokes given and returned on both sides, Saint Croix gave Azevedo a vigorous thrust in the face. Azevedo took his sword from him very skilfully, and plunged his own in St. Croix's thigh downwards, cutting him to the bone. The blood spouted out, and St. Croix took but one step, and fell. Azevedo cried out to him, "Give yourself up, St. Croix, or I shall slay you;" but, without answering, he

---

[1] The Loyal Servant adds, "*two secrettes*" as well as the rapiers and the poniards, and we learn from Du Cange that the *secrette* was a small but very effective axe. See Glossary, vol. vi. p. 314, at the word *secures*.

still sat on the ground with the sword in his hand, and made passes as if he still fought.

Azevedo begged him to get up, saying that he would not strike him while he was down. St. Croix tried, but he only took two steps, and then fell on his face, when his opponent raised his sword to cut off his head, which would have been easy to do; but he did not strike.

The Duchess of Ferrara, frightened at this horrible sight, begged the Duke of Nemours to separate the combatants.

"I cannot do it in honour, madam," said he to her. "Right gives the conquered to the victor." However, St. Croix lost all his blood, and yet would not give himself up. The prior of Messina went to Azevedo, and said to him, "My lord, I know the heart of St. Croix, and that he would only give up to death. I give myself up for him as his second." Then they called the surgeon to dress the wound, and stop the blood, after which his people carried him off in their arms. The conqueror threw himself on his knees to thank God for having given him the victory, and was led in triumph to the Duke of Nemours' house by those who had accompanied him.

By the law of victory the arms of St. Croix should belong to Azevedo, so he sent to demand them; but they refused them. He complained of this to the Duke of Ferrara, who charged the knight Bayard to go and demand them, and make them give them up; that otherwise St. Croix should be brought back to the field, his wound undressed, and his person abandoned to the discretion of the conqueror The severity of these conditions settled the matter, and his arms were given up.

But it is time to return to our history. After the pope's troops had been driven from the Duchy of

Ferrara, they joined themselves to those of Spain. They then came with the intention of besieging Bologna, which siege they were speedily forced to raise. The Venetians, on the other side, were besieging Verona, where the Lord of Plessis was in command for the king. This place had been given by the emperor to the king as hostage for a considerable loan of money. The grandmaster went to its assistance, and had the siege raised, as he had done at Bologna. This was his last exploit; a short time after he died in the little town of Corregion at the early age of thirty-eight. He had been appointed Governor of Milan at twenty-five, and for thirteen years had kept his master's Italian states with the wisdom and prudence of an experienced man. He was a nephew worthy of the Cardinal of Amboise, who had adorned him with the offices of grandmaster, marshal, and admiral of France, as we have already said.[2] The tears of all the officers, the soldiers, and the people were his praise, and the regrets of the king and all the kingdom were a sufficient renown.

---

[2] He was the son of Charles d'Amboise, Lord of Chaumont, Governor of Burgundy and Champagne, and grandson of Peter, father of the Cardinal George, and seven other sons. All this large and numerous house is extinct; the name alone is preserved by the alliance of the heiress with a member of the house of Clermont Gallerande, whose cadet branch, known by the name of Clermont of Amboise, exists in the person of John Baptist Louis, Marquis of Resnel, called the Marquis of Clermont, lieutenant-general of the king's armies, who is appointed to the name and arms of Amboise. He has an only son, Dom d'Aubrac in Rouergue, a knight of Malta. Again, there are two houses which join to their name that of Amboise, the Marquis of Aubijoux, and a branch of the house of Crussol. The arms of the Marquis of Clermont are azure, three chevrons or, that of the chief broken at the point, quartered with those of Amboise, which are pallé or, and gules in six pieces.

Louis immediately sent the Duke of Longueville to replace him in his post of lieutenant-general. Longueville did nothing but renew the oath of allegiance to the king and to Madame Claude of France, his eldest daughter, sworn by all those who held places in the Duchy of Milan. After that he returned, and was immediately succeeded by the Duke of Nemours, with all the authority that the grandmaster himself had had.

At the end of the same year—that is to say, towards Christmas—the Duke of Nemours learned that a large troop of Swiss were descending into the duchy of Milan to drive him from it. He went to meet them with the few men that remained with him, but the greater part of his soldiers were in winter quarters, or in garrison at Verona, Bologna, and other places. Not finding their numbers sufficiently large to oppose so vast a body of men, they were obliged to return to Milan, and had the misfortune to lose the Baron of Conti, who was mortally wounded in the retreat, and died soon after. His death was avenged with interest the next day by the baron's good friend, Bayard, our noble hero, who left 500 Swiss dead on the field where Conti had been wounded. This disgrace and want of provisions forced their leader, the Baron of Saxony, to enter into a negotiation with the Duke of Nemours, and in consequence of this they returned to their own country, but not before they had left cruel traces of their visit, and had burnt about twenty large villages on their road. The Duke of Nemours, rid of the Swiss, had scarcely breathing time, when he learnt that the Spaniards were approaching Bologna to besiege it. He set out with his army for Final, and established his quarters in its environs. On the road from Milan to Final he remained two days in the little town of Carpi, with the heads of his army, and those whom he loved and trusted. This town belonged to Albert Pico, Count of Carpi, cousin-german to John Francis Pico, Count of La Mirandola, both of them noted for their learning.

The count made great cheer for the chief and French captains, and amongst other things they had the amusement of an astrologer, who was then in the town, whose history is curious enough to merit a place here.[3]

This astrologer was a little withered black man, of about sixty years of age, who astonished all the world by the tales he told every one of things which had happened to them, without having had any previous knowledge of their history, and still more by his predictions, which results had often verified. When the Duke of Nemours and all his company had heard the history of this man, they wished to see him, and amuse themselves with him. They sent word to him to present himself before the count. When he arrived, the duke spoke to him in a friendly manner, and asked him several questions on indifferent subjects before coming to the point. He asked him if the Viceroy of Naples and the Spanish expected battle, to which he answered yes; that by his head[4] battle would be given on Good Friday or Easter

---

[3] "It certainly ought to be acknowledged,"—says the Loyal Servant, wiser in his generation than Lieutenant Morrison (Zadkiel), and those who consult his almanac, are in this,—" by all true Christians that God alone can see into futurity; yet this astrologer of Carpi said so many things and to so many different people, which afterwards proved true, that he turned the heads of a number."

[4] "Cursed be the hour," says the Loyal Servant, while relating this singular story, "alas! whereof he prophesied so truly." The Duke of Nemours, who in these chronicles is always referred to as gentle, good, and kind, seems to have been sincerely loved by all those about him.

Day, and that there would be much bloodshed. The duke asked him again who would gain it. His answer was, that the field would remain to the French, that the Spaniards would lose more there than they had ever lost in one battle before; but that the loss of the French would be as great on account of the number and quality of the brave men they would leave there. He surprised everybody by the assurance of his answers and the good sense which he showed.

Chabannes asked him if he were among those who would die at that time.

"No," said the little man, "you have still a dozen years to live, but you will die in another battle."

He said as much to the Lord of Humbercourt, and announced to the Captain Richebourg that he was doomed to perish by lightning. Finally, all the company questioned him, and he answered all very wisely and pertinently. Bayard laughed at him, or rather mocked him, but the Duke of Nemours wished that he also should question the astrologer as to his future. The knight answered him, laughing, that he did not mind the trouble of questioning him, but that he knew well enough without asking that he should never become a great man. However, he spoke to the astrologer.

"My master," said he, "tell me if I shall be a man of consequence some day, and if I shall become rich?"

The other, after scanning his face and looking in his hand, according to custom, answered him, "You shall be richer in honour and virtue than ever French captain was before you, but you shall have scarcely any of fortune's goods, so do not seek them. You shall serve another King of France besides the one who now reigns, and whom you serve, who will love and esteem you much; but the envy of those surrounding him will prevent his giving you great riches, or promoting you to the honour that your merit will have deserved: always believe that the fault will not be his."

"But," replied Bayard, "shall I escape from this battle, which you declare will be so bloody?"

"Yes," replied the oracle; "but a dozen years hence, at the most, you will die in action, and of a cannon shot; in no other way, for you stand first in the hearts of all your soldiers, who would die to the last man to save your life."

After he had answered everybody's questions, perceiving that the Duke of Nemours was more friendly to Chabannes and Bayard than to any of the others, he drew them on one side, and said to them, "Your prince over there appears to be very dear to you; he deserves it. I have never seen such a happy countenance; but take care of him on the day of battle; I see that he is threatened to remain there. I am almost sure that he will die there, but if he escapes he will be one of the greatest men that France has yet produced."

These proceedings were interrupted by the arrival of an adventurer, an ensign in Captain Molart's band. This man, named Jacquin Caumont, was a brave soldier, but coarse and vicious. He also wished to take part in the amusement, and know his good fortune.

"Come here," he said to the astrologer in insolent tones, "and tell me my good fortune."

Caumont was rebuked by the nobles for his bad manners: they made him apologize to the astrologer, and told him to question him more civilly if he wanted to know anything. The old man was annoyed at first, and would not reply to him; but he relented, and after examining his face and hands, he said, "Do not ask me anything, for I have nothing but bad fortune for you."

Caumont pressed him to tell him what it was.

"If you will know, I must tell you," said the astrologer. "Look to your conscience quickly, for in less than three months from this, you shall be hanged till you are dead."

All the company laughed immoderately at this prediction, but it was verified shortly afterwards, as we shall see; also Bayard's death in 1524, that of Humbercourt in 1522, and that of Chabannes in 1525.

What we have just related happened at the end of January, 1511, at Carpi, whence the Duke of Nemours went to Final; and from there, awaiting news of the Spanish army, he went to spend a few days at Ferrara. On returning to his camp, he learnt that it was time to go to Bologna in all diligence, for that otherwise the town and garrison would be lost. He assembled his captains together, and held a council of war with them, when it was resolved to set out without losing a moment to raise the siege. This they did, and the first news that greeted them on their arrival at Bologna was to the effect that the Venetians had entered again into Brescia by surprise, as we shall proceed to relate.

CHAPTER XVI.

BRESCIA is one of the most beautiful towns in Europe. Strong, rich, and remarkably well situated, its climate is delightful, and its soil fertile in all that is necessary to support life. Three valleys, one stretching out from Germany and the other two from Friuli, join in its territory, and by one or the other of these valleys the town can always be supplied with men and provisions.

The King of France had been master of it since May, 1509, and had placed the Count of Lude there as Governor, and a Biscayan gentleman named Hérigoye as captain of the castle. The Venetians wished for nothing so much as the re-capture of this place, not only because of its importance, but also because from there they could cut off provisions from Verona, and oppose any convoys that might come from Milan. Of course, having once possessed the town, they had many friends within its walls, but no one dared stretch out a helping hand to them, for the late Baron of Conti and the knight Bayard had once beheaded one of their magnates, the Count of Martineugne, for preparing a surprise for them, and this deterred the inhabitants from again attempting to assist them. But what the Venetians never hoped to attain by force of arms, or spies, or treason, a quarrel between two youngsters brought about, and occasioned their re-entering Brescia, and the slaughter of a great number of French. So true is it that great events often spring from small causes.

The Count of Gambara and the Count Louis Avogara were two of the principal nobles of the town. Each had a son of about the same age, who one day quarrelled and fought. Gambara, a little stronger than his opponent, wounded him dangerously. The Count Avogara knew not how to be revenged, so he went to Milan to demand justice of the Duke of Nemours; but whether the wounded man was in the wrong, or whether the Duke of Nemours, being occupied with more important matters, had not time to attend to his case, certain it is that Avogara did not get satisfaction, and his anger led him to revenge himself upon all the French at the risk of what might happen to himself. He dissembled for some time, and then, pretending to go into the country on business, he went to Venice, and held a conference with the Doge and the councillors, and explained his plot and the means of executing it.

They entirely agreed with him, and promised that on the day named, the provéditore, Andrea Gritti, should be before the town with from 7000 to 8000 men, and a number of armed peasants from the mountains. Avogara returned to Brescia, and managed to persuade the principal inhabitants of the town of the justice of his cause, and the plot was crowned with the greatest success. The Count de Lude was always on the watch, but he had not enough soldiers to resist a general revolt. On the appointed day the Venetian army came to give the alarm at one of the gates, and while they were occupied in defending it, a party of troops broke the iron bars of a drain at the other end of the town, and entered in a great number, crying, "Marco! Marco!" At this signal the Count Avogara and all his accomplices appeared in arms, and placed the garrison between two fires, and immediately the gates were opened to the troops without. The Count of Lude, seeing himself surprised and betrayed, sounded the retreat, and retired as best he could to the castle, abandoning horses, arms, and baggage. All those belonging to the garrison found within the town were murdered; they did not deign to take a single prisoner. The Count of Gambara found the means to save himself, and very fortunately, for as soon as his enemy saw himself the stronger the first thing that he did was to go to all the houses belonging to the family of Gambara, and to plunder and burn them.

The conqueror, feeling that it was useless to have the town without the castle, sent a trumpet to summon those who were inside to give themselves up; but the brave men they had to do with made no reply, although from their large number their provisions could not last long. However, the provéditore cannonaded the castle vigorously, and made a large breach. He had two large machines made of wood, capable of containing 100 men, to approach the breach.

The Count of Lude had found means to send a man to the Duke of Nemours. The messenger had the good fortune to get away safely, although all the approaches were well guarded. He informed the duke of what had happened, and told him that if he did not send assistance to the Count of Lude, the castle could not hold out more than eight days. The siege of Bologna had just been raised and the Spaniards beaten, and the duke was so grieved at the loss of Brescia that he determined to go and retake it. He called his captains together, and informed them of the sad event, and they quite agreed with him that they could not afford to lose this beautiful and interesting Italian possession of theirs. They considered that the re-capture would be easy, provided that the castle held out till their arrival, and without losing any time they set out at once for Brescia.

The Provéditore Gritti was not idle. He had no doubt that as soon as the Duke of Nemours heard of the capture of this place he would hasten to take it. He wrote with all speed to the Seignory of Venice to inform them of the success that he had had, and spoke of the danger he should be in if a large French army arrived, that his forces were not large enough to await it in the town, much less to give battle to it; that on the keeping of Brescia depended the retaking of all the places that they had lost; and he concluded with a wish that they would speedily send him assistance sufficiently powerful to put him in a position to profit by his victory.

The Seignory was too well satisfied at this first success not to try to push it farther. Orders were sent to the Captain-General John Paul Baillon to march night and day to Brescia with 400 men-at-arms and 4000 foot-soldiers. Baillon executed the order of the republic without delay; but the Duke of Nemours, as diligent as he, so hastened his march that his men got over as much ground in the day as a body of cavalry would have been able to do, and he arrived first at a castle named Valège, which the Venetian general wished to make himself master of before entering Brescia, and where there was a French garrison. The time that the Venetian lost there made him miss that which was worth having, and gave to the French the means of gaining the town before him, and of attacking him in a narrow defile.

The Venetians took with them six pieces of artillery, which they fired upon the French vanguard, led by Bayard and another valiant captain, a standard-bearer of Téligny's company, who was killed there.

Bayard, who had had the ague all the night, and who was on horseback in his night-gown,[1] seeing himself alone entrusted with the attack, put on the corslet of an adventurer, then mounted an excellent horse, and, followed by Téligny, without waiting for the greater part of his vanguard, which was still at a distance, charged the enemy with his ordinary valour, and held out against them for a quarter of an hour, notwithstanding the inequality of numbers. He was soon joined by his troop; but the Venetian general had no sooner seen them assembled than he turned his back with so much speed that those who pursued him could not reach him. However, all his foot-soldiers, and nearly all his men-at-arms, remained upon the field with his artillery. News of this happy event, due to the knight Bayard alone, was soon taken to the French camp, and caused general rejoicing both there and at the castle, which, by continual firing, testified its joy.

The Duke of Nemours and the captains regretted that they were not present during these proceedings, but they were not at all jealous of our hero; the admir-

---

[1] In his night-gown; that is, not as we now understand it, but in a velvet robe de chambre. "He was not armed, but had on a black velvet riding dress," says the Loyal Servant. It was such a gown as Hamlet wore when, rising in the night, he discovered the treachery of Guildenstern and Rosencrantz:—

"Up from my cabin,
My sea-gown scarf'd about me."—Act v. sc. ii.

ation they had for him was mixed with no shade of envy.

The inhabitants of Brescia were in a general consternation, foreseeing what must happen sooner or later. They begged the provéditore, Messer Andrea Gritti, to leave their town that they might give it up to the French; but he refused them constantly, and finally repented that he had done so.

The Duke of Nemours, who was still twenty miles from the town when the Venetians were defeated, went the following day to the foot of the castle, having met in a village on the road a number of Venetian foot-soldiers, who tried to stand their ground, but were speedily cut in pieces. On his arrival, several of the French captains went to the castle to reassure the Count of Lude and the Captain Hérigoye, who, by way of rejoicing, sent about twenty volleys of cannon amongst the townspeople, to whom this sort of joy was doubtless anything but pleasing. The next day the prince and all the captains assembled at the castle, and there determined to give a general assault to the town.

The French general knew that there were about 8000 regular troops, and 12,000 or 14,000 peasants or militiamen in the town, which was well fortified, whilst he had only about 12,000 men in all. These, however, were picked troops, as the surplus had remained at Bologna. They went down, without trouble, from the castle to the town. There were no ditches which crossed the marsh, but a tolerably good newly-made rampart. All being thus arranged, and every one showing the greatest ardour, joined to the confidence and friendship which they had for the Duke of Nemours, the assault was ordered for nine o'clock in the morning on the following day. The plan was, that the Lord of Molard should lead the first, that the Captain Hérigoye, with his foot-soldiers, should begin to skirmish; after him should come the Captain Jacob with the 2000 lansquenets that he commanded, and after him Bonnet, Maugiron, the bastard of Clèves, and others, with their men, amounting to 7000 in all; that the duke with the gentlemen under the orders of the Seneschal of Normandy, and the greater part of the men-at-arms, all on foot and fully armed, should march by the side of the 7000 men before named; that last of all D'Alègre with 300 horses should post himself at the gate of St. John (which was the only one remaining open, all the others being walled up), and hinder people from leaving the town.

Chabannes was not able to be there, having been wounded in the head the day before by a piece of stone splintered by a cannon ball fired at the castle from the town. This plan of attack was agreed to by every one but Bayard, who was not quite satisfied with it. He considered that as the Lord of Molard was to lead the attack, he would have all the picked men of the enemy to resist, "and as in this position," said he, "he cannot possibly retreat (as I am sure he would not think of doing), I advise that he shall have 150 men-at-arms to support his foot-soldiers."

"What you say is very just and true," replied the Duke of Nemours, "but what captain would put himself at the mercy of their arquebuses?"

"I will," replied Bayard, "if you approve of the plan, and I will answer for it that the company I command will do such honour and service to the king as shall be well worthy of appreciation."

Every one looked at his neighbour in astonishment at this dangerous proposition; but Bayard was persistent, and no one was inclined to dispute his commission with him. Everything being thus settled, the Duke of Nemours, touched with the fate of the poor inhabitants who were going to be sacked and massacred, thought they ought to make one more effort to save the town and its people from the evils they would otherwise have to undergo, and to see if they would give themselves up.

This kindness was much approved of, and it was agreed that before the attack on the next day they should send a herald to summon the townspeople to a parley. This was done. The herald began sounding his trumpet at the gate of the town, and went on thus to the rampart, where he found the Provéditore Gritti, and all the captains, who, without allowing him to enter the town, received his message, which was, that if they chose to give up the town their lives should be spared ; that otherwise, if they sustained a siege, they must all expect nothing short of death.

The answer was, that the town belonged to the Seignory of Venice, that it wished still to remain in the possesssion of that power, and that no Frenchman should put foot inside it as long as they were on guard. The inhabitants thought very differently, and would willingly have given themselves up; but they were not consulted. The herald went up to the castle with his answer. The Duke of Nemours, who in the interval had settled the whole order of battle, cried, "Let us go, then, my friends and companions; in the name of God and St. Denis let us show them what we can do." At that moment he caused such a noise of clarions and trumpets, and drums to be made, that it was enough to make the hair of the boldest stand on end. The enemy, hearing this noise, answered with many volleys of cannon shot, one of which went right into the midst of the duke's company, but happily without killing or wounding one man.

The march was headed, as had been settled, by the Captains Molard and Hérigoye with their men, Bayard with his men-at-arms forming the two wings. The gentlemen of Bayard's company were all picked men, and noble and valiant soldiers. The greater number of them had been commanders themselves, but preferred the honour of serving under Bayard to having troops of their own to command. These troops reached the first rampart, behind which were their enemies, who defended the approach with their artillery and arquebuses, which strewed shot like hail amongst the French.

Both sides fought like lions, the French crying, "France! France! Bayard! Bayard!" and those in the town, "Marco! Marco!" with noise enough to drown the roar of the cannon.

The Provéditore Gritti, to encourage his men, said to them, "Hold fast, comrades. The French have only the first rush; they will be tired presently, and if this Bayard were defeated, all the rest would lose heart." However, the attack became increasingly furious on both sides. The French began to drive back the Venetians, and made them retreat a little. Bayard, perceiving it, cried, "Courage, companions; let us go in, they are ours." The good knight was the first to cross the rampart, and was soon followed by his whole troop, to the number of more than a thousand, who gained the first fort; but it cost both sides much blood, the French, however, much less than the Venetians. Bayard, especially, paid dearly for the honour he had gained in leaping the rampart. He received such a terrible pike thrust in the top of his thigh that a spear-head remained broken short off in his flesh. The pain he felt was so great that he thought he was dying. "Captain Molard," he said, "take the command of my men; the town is gained, but I shall never enter it. I am wounded to the death." The blood was streaming from his wound, and two of his men tore up their shirts to staunch it, and then carried him out of the fray as quietly as they could.

But the Lord of Molard, furious at the loss of his men, swore, with tears in his eyes, that he would have vengeance, and he and his whole troop threw themselves upon their enemies, like tigers upon their prey, and overthrew all who came in their way. The Duke of Nemours, learning that the first fort was taken, but that Bayard was mortally wounded, felt as much grief as if he himself had received the blow. "Let us go, my friends and comrades," he cried, "let us go and avenge the death *of the most accomplished knight that ever lived.* Follow me."

On his arrival, the Venetians, already driven back, left the rampart, and, with the idea of re-entering the town, tried to raise the bridge, which would have been a great hindrance to the French; but they fortunately had no time to do what they intended; the French pursued them so quickly that they all entered together pell-mell, and arriving in this manner in the great square, found all the cavalry and infantry ranged ready for battle. The lansquenets and the French foot-soldiers were very brave, and distinguished themselves particularly by their feats of valour.

Captain Bonnet commenced the attack, which was furious indeed. The poor French had not only to fight against the men, but to stand the attacks of the women of the town, who from the windows of the houses threw stones, bricks, boiling water, and pieces of furniture upon them. In this battle, which scarcely lasted half an hour, the Venetians were totally defeated. From 7000 to 8000 lay dead in the square, and the rest sought safety in flight: but from street to street they met soldiers, who gave them no quarter. The provéditore, the Count Avogara, author of the treason, and all the captains, seeing the rout become general, ran towards the gate of St. John, crying "Marco!" and had the bridge lowered; but they were driven back by D'Alègre and his 300 men-at-arms, who charged them so vigorously that they overthrew them nearly all. The provéditore, seeing himself pursued, took refuge in a house, where he was made prisoner with Avogara. Such a terrible and complete carnage had not been seen for a long time. The Venetians reckoned their dead at above 20,000 men, soldiers and townspeople, while the French did not lose fifty. Afterwards the French began the pillage of the place, which was immense, and the desire for which carried them even unto the convents, where the soldiers gave themselves up to all sorts of excesses. But the great value of the plunder was a misfortune for the French, for the soldiers, being enriched by it, deserted in bands, and returned to their homes, which left the army much weakened, and in a short time led to the loss of all the places the French held in Italy.

Bayard, mortally wounded, as he supposed, at the beginning of the action, was placed by two of his soldiers on a wooden gate, which they took from the first house they came to; and having withdrawn him from the crowd, they carried him into a beautiful large house at a little distance, belonging to a gentleman who had deserted it, leaving his wife and two young and beautiful daughters to the care of Providence. The lady her-

self opened the gate, and received Bayard as a dying
man. He ordered his two soldiers to station themselves
at the gate, and on pain of death not to admit any but
his men.

"I am sure," said he to the men, "that when they
know I am lodged here they will not force a passage;
and I will indemnify you for your loss of the plunder."

His two soldiers, led by the lady, carried him into a
beautiful apartment, and as soon as they arrived there
she threw herself on her knees, and spoke to him in
these words:—"Noble lord, I offer you this house and
all that it contains; all is yours by the laws of war. I
only ask you one favour, which is that you will preserve
the lives and honour of myself and my two daughters."

"Madam," said Bayard, scarcely able to speak, "I
do not know whether I shall recover from the wound I
have received, but as long as I live neither you nor
your daughters shall sustain more injury than myself;
only take care of them, and do not let them appear. I
promise you that no one shall enter the house contrary
to your wish. I am not the man to plunder you; on
the contrary, I promise you all the respect and friendship in my power. But the most urgent need now is to
procure me some help, and that quickly."

The lady, relieved by the knight's words, went herself, accompanied by one of his soldiers, to look for a
surgeon who lived two houses distant from her. As
soon as he arrived he examined the wound, which was
large and deep, but happily, as he declared, not mortal.
He applied the first dressing, and when that was removed, the Duke of Nemours sent his surgeon, with
orders not to leave the invalid. Indeed, the surgeon
treated him so well that in less that a month and a half
he was fit to get on horseback.

As soon as Bayard's wound was dressed, he asked his hostess where her husband was.

"I don't know," she replied, weeping bitterly, "whether he is dead or alive, but I believe he has taken refuge in a convent, where he has many friends."

"Try to find out, madam," said Bayard, "and I will promise you to have him brought home in safety."

When they learnt the place of his retreat, Bayard sent his maître d'hôtel with two archers, who accompanied him into the sick man's room, by whom he was received with a good grace; and the assurances of safety and protection that had been given to the lady were renewed to him. We shall see that Bayard kept his word to them even more strictly than they could have hoped.

After the glorious but bloody re-capture of Brescia by the French, the Duke of Nemours' first care was to establish order as far as possible. He began by sending orders that all the soldiers were to leave the churches and convents, and that the inhabitants of the town were to return to their homes; next he gave orders that the dead bodies should be taken outside the town. The number was found to exceed 22,000. He filled up the officers' places which had become vacant, and did all that prudence dictated to restore good order everywhere, after which he brought the Count Avogara, and Thomas Del Duca, and Jerôme de Rive, his principal accomplices, to trial. They were condemned to be beheaded and afterwards quartered.

During the seven or eight days that the duke remained in the town he did not allow one to pass without going to see our hero once or twice, and encouraging him to get well quickly. "Because," said he, "we shall be obliged to give battle to the Spaniards in a month from this time, and I would give all the world for your presence at that time."

"If you desire my presence there," replied Bayard, "I assure you I should like nothing better, and, God helping me, I will be there, even if I am carried in a litter."

The duke, before leaving the town, made Bayard many presents; amongst other things he gave him 500 crowns, which he divided between his two soldiers, having promised that he would make up to them for the loss of their share of the plunder.

When the king learnt that the town of Brescia had been reduced to submission, he felt very great joy, and wished more strongly than ever to pursue the victory, and to drive the Spaniards entirely from Lombardy, for he judged that, as long as they were there, his state of Milan would never be in safety. He wrote letter after letter to his nephew, the Duke of Nemours, who saw the matter in the same light as he did. The king told him, amongst other things, that he could not defray the expenses of the foot-soldiers whom he had hired without levying taxes on his people, which he feared doing more than anything else in the world; and he added that he knew the King of England meditated a descent upon some province of France; that the Swiss on their side had evil designs upon the country; and he always concluded by wishing the Spaniards sent so far away that they should never return again.

The duke, as well to obey the king as because he himself saw the necessity for a battle which might put an end to the war, set out from Brescia with all his captains and horse and foot-soldiers, and went to Bologna, where the Duke of Ferrara arrived soon after, and, in conjunction with Chabannes, was entrusted with the charge of the vanguard. The French met the Spanish army at a few miles from Bologna. It was one of the finest armies on record, not only from the number, but the superiority of its troops, and on account of the richness of the equipments and the beauty of the horses. Don Raymond of Cardona, the viceroy of Naples, was commander-in-chief; he had in his own particular company 1200 or 1400 men-at-arms, armed cap-à-pied; besides these he had 12,000 foot-soldiers—that is to say, 2000 Italians, under the orders of a captain named Ramessot, and 10,000 Spaniards, Biscayans, or Neapolitans, commanded by Don Pedro of Navarre, who had formerly led these troops into Barbary, where they had gained him two or three battles. All these troops were accomplished soldiers, and men to be trusted. They had for two years done nothing but wander about Lombardy, which is a country abundant in provisions and pasturage, and where both men and horses had had everything they could desire.

For three or four weeks the two armies kept continually at five or six miles from each other. The Spaniards took care to encamp themselves to their advantage, and often skirmished with the French, sometimes one party, sometimes the other, gaining the advantage.

But notwithstanding the situation of the Spaniards, and the flourishing state of their army, the French were very desirous of seeing them in open field, so that they might give battle to them. This desirable occasion was not long in presenting itself, as we shall show, after having seen how Bayard recovered from his wound, and with what generosity he treated his hosts.

CHAPTER XVII.

HE good knight, who was believed to be mortally wounded, had been allowed to leave his room after five or six weeks, and his wound got daily better, although not so quickly as he wished. He was uneasy as the time approached for the battle which the duke had resolved to fight with the Spaniards, for he would not have missed his chance of being there for all the gold in the world.

His impatience at last induced him to try his strength; he got up and walked about the room a little. His courage was greater than his weakness, and he sent for his surgeon to ask him if he were in a fit state to get into the saddle once more.

"It seems to me," said he, "that I am well; and I assure you that I should be worse if made to keep my room, than if I were allowed to go to the field."

The surgeon, who knew him, assured him that the wound was internally healed, and it was only necessary to leave it for the scar to heal, and he added, "Your valet can do all you want; he has seen me dress your wound, and as I intend giving him the ointment which I used, he will be able to dress it as well as I could."

Bayard, transported with joy, rewarded the surgeon

with his usual liberality, and, having resolved to depart in two days, ordered his men to get ready to accompany him in that time.

The gentleman and lady in whose house he was, hearing of his approaching departure, and considering that themselves, their children, and their property (which might have been as much as 2000 gold ducats[1] a year) belonged to him, were in doubt as to how he would treat them, and fully expected that they should have to pay him at least 10,000 ducats for ransom. The lady, who had reason to know the nobility of his sentiments, hoped that he would content himself with the offer she would make him. She put 2500 golden ducats in a little highly ornamented steel coffer, and on the morning of the day of Bayard's departure she entered his room, followed by a lacquey carrying the coffer. She began by throwing herself on her knees, but the good knight forced her to rise, and would not listen to her until she was seated near him.

"My lord," she said, "I shall thank God all my life that it pleased him, in the midst of the sacking of our town, to lead such a generous knight to our house; and my husband and children shall always look upon you as our tutelar angel, and shall ever remember that it is to you we owe our lives and our honour. Ever since you came amongst us, we have received from you nothing but proofs of goodness and friendship. Your men even have treated us with respect, and have taken nothing from us without payment. We confess we are your prisoners; the house, with all it contains, is yours by right of con-

---

[1] It was a very small piece of money of the size and value of the present sequin, which is worth about 11 francs 10 sous French money.

quest; but you have shown us such generosity and greatness of mind that I have come to beg you to have pity on us, and to be satisfied with the little present that I have the honour to offer you."

So saying, she opened the coffer, and showed Bayard its contents. The knight, who never in his life had set any value upon either gold or silver, smiled and said to her, "How much have you there?"

The lady, thinking that he was speaking contemptuously, and that he considered the present too small, answered him, trembling all the time, "My lord, there are only 2500 ducats; but if you are not satisfied, mention the sum you wish to have, and we will try to get it."

"That is not what I was going to say," replied Bayard. "If you were to offer me 100,000 ducats, I should not value them as much as all the kindness you have shown me since I have been with you, and the company you have borne me, both yourself and your whole family. Instead of taking your money, I promise you that as long as I live you shall find me always ready to serve you and be your friend, and I shall ever hold dear the remembrance of your benefits."

The lady, much astonished at this reply, which she had not in the least expected, threw herself on her knees, with tears in her eyes, to beg him to accept her present.

"I shall consider myself the most unhappy woman in the world," said she, "if you refuse it, and I shall think we have not deserved all the goodness you have shown us while you have been here."

"As you wish it so much," replied Bayard, "I accept it; but I pray you send your daughters here that I may take leave of them."

While she was gone to call them, Bayard divided the ducats into three lots—two of 1000 ducats each, and the other of 500. The young girls having come, the first thing they did was to throw themselves on their knees; but he made them get up, and seat themselves. Then the elder of them said to him, "You see before you, my lord, two young girls who owe their lives and honour to you. We are very sorry not to be able to show our thanks otherwise than by praying to God for you all our lives, and asking Him to reward you both in this world and the next."

Bayard, affected almost to tears, thanked them for their help and their charming society, for they had been his daily companions, and amused him by working in his room, and singing or playing on the lute to him.

"You know," said he, "that soldiers are not ordinarily loaded with jewels or other things to present to young ladies; but your mother has just compelled me to accept from her 2500 ducats that you see there. I give you a thousand each to form part of your marriage portions;" and in spite of their protestations he made them accept his gifts, asking nothing in return but their prayers to God for him. Then addressing himself to the mother, "Madam," said he, "these 500 ducats remain to me, and I intend to distribute them amongst the poor convents which have suffered most from the pillage; and as I am about to leave, and as you are more likely than I am to know who have the greatest need of relief, I leave this work to you, and I must now take leave of you and your daughters."

They again fell on their knees, sobbing as if they had lost their father. They pressed his hands in theirs, and the mother, so moved that she could scarcely utter her words, said to him, "Too generous knight, God alone can reward your virtues. We will daily pray to Him without ceasing to spare your life."

After this, she retired with her daughters. Bayard sent to beg the father to come and dine with him. Having been informed of what had passed, he entered the room, and with one knee on the ground, began outpouring his thanks, and offers of his services, his property, and his person. As soon as they had dined, Bayard, who had ordered his carriages to be ready, prepared to set out, when the two young ladies came to him, and begged him to accept from each a piece of her work. The elder of the two gave him two pretty bracelets of gold and silver-thread, and the other a crimson satin purse, beautifully embroidered. He was as grateful to them as if they had given him a fortune, put on the two bracelets in their presence, and put the purse in his pocket, promising the young ladies that as long as their presents lasted, he would wear them. The farewells and tears began again, but the separation was a thing of necessity, and while they were yet bitterly grieving at his departure, Bayard left them.

CHAPTER XVIII.

HE knight took the road to the camp before Bologna, accompanied by his good friend, the Lord d'Aubigny, whom the Duke of Nemours had left governor at Brescia, and who led him with a great number of gentlemen to within two or three miles of his destination. Some of them followed him to the camp, where they arrived the Wednesday before Easter. Bayard was received by the prince and all the army with such great demonstrations of joy that it seemed as if he alone were a reinforcement of 10,000 men. The camp was that day before Ravenna. The Spaniards were six miles' distant, but the next day they approached to within two miles of the French. The day after Bayard's arrival the Duke of Nemours held a council of war upon the plan which it would be wisest to pursue. He showed how the French army had begun to suffer for want of provisions, that bread and wine would soon be wanting, because the Venetians on one side and the Spaniards on the other, occupied the passages of the Romagna. But he did not know, neither did any of his officers, another inconvenience that interested him equally—namely, that the emperor had ordered, by letter, the captains of the lansquenets to

retire on pain of their heads, immediately his orders were received. By good fortune, these letters were given to two men, too generous to use them. Of these one was Philip of Friberg, and the other the Captain Jacob, of whom we have already spoken, who had formerly received benefits from Louis XII, so that his heart was more French than German. He had contracted a singular friendship for Bayard ever since the emperor's expedition to Padua in 1509. He had no sooner received the letter than hearing of Bayard's arrival at the camp, he went to see him without any other witness but his interpreter (never having been able to learn the French language). After many mutual protestations of friendship, he informed the knight of the emperor's orders, of which none but he and Friberg had any knowledge. He protested that, having given his oath to the king, and being in his pay, he would sooner die a thousand times than be so unfaithful to him, though he was very certain that if the lansquenets were informed of the order, not one of them would fight. He said how necessary it was to hasten matters, for fear the emperor should send new orders, more especially because the lansquenets formed the third part of the army.

Bayard thanked him very heartily for the good service he had rendered to the king, on whose part he promised him any reward he might expect, " although," added he, " I am the only man to give him an account of it. Let us go to our general, the Duke of Nemours. He is now holding a council, and we will declare to him what you have just told me."

When they arrived, opinions were divided. Some had good reasons why battle should not be given ; others had good reasons why it should be, and that immediately. The first said, "If we lose it, which is possible, all Italy is lost to the king, and not one of us will escape. We shall have to cross three or four rivers in our retreat, and we have enemies on all sides—the pope, the Venetians, the Spaniards, and the Swiss, and we can trust but little to the emperor."

The others said, "Our position forces us to give battle, or to die with hunger like wretches and cowards. We have gone too far to retreat otherwise than in disorder, and covered with shame."

The Duke of Nemours, already informed by Bayard of what had brought him there with the Captain Jacob, was urgent for the battle, and presented the letters of the king, his uncle, which arrived daily, because of the fear he was in of being attacked in his kingdom on all sides at once. However, the duke asked the advice of Bayard, who, without mentioning the secret he knew, answered, "I only arrived yesterday, my lord, so I do not know the enemy's forces as my comrades do, who have been near enough to skirmish with them; but as you ask my advice, and I have heard that some are in favour of battle, and others against it, I may tell them that it is always dangerous to give battle, and perhaps very much so in this instance, on account of your situation; one ought not to expose oneself to it without much prudence. However, taking into consideration the state of the enemy and our own, I think you ought to give battle, because you have already made your approaches before Ravenna, and to-morrow you ought to cannonade it, in order to give the assault as soon as the breach is made. You know that the Lord Marc Antony Colonna, who has been here more than thirteen days, only entered here on the word and oath of the Viceroy of Naples, general of the Spaniards, of the

Lord Fabricius Colonna, his uncle, of Don Pedro of
Navarre, and all the captains, to give him help, if he
can wait till to-morrow, or at the latest till Easter-day.
You know, also, that they have the power to keep their
word, since they are close upon our army; besides, we
shall not be able to remain in the position in which we
are now, and we shall want provisions and forage, and
the king presses you to give battle as the only means of
keeping, not only his duchy of Milan, but his whole
kingdom, for the causes which he writes to you, so I
conclude that we must fight, and endeavour to act wisely,
for we have a large and fine army at stake. But one
thing comforts me. For two years the Spaniards have
done little else but eat and drink; they are so stout
and unwieldy that they are not active, whereas our
men have known what it was to want food, and will have
better breath, and I assure you that the field will remain
to the side which fights longest."

This remark made every one laugh, but it was none
the less sensible for that. The Lords of Lautrec,
Chabannes,[1] Crussol, the grand seneschal of Normandy,
and nearly all the captains ranged themselves on Bayard's
side, and on the spot all the officers of the gendarmes and
foot-soldiers had orders to prepare to give battle.

The next day, which was Good Friday, the town of
Ravenna was so vigorously cannonaded that the Spaniards could count each separate discharge in their
camp, so they prepared for their duty of helping the
town, as they had engaged to do. They answered from
the chief square to the cannon of the French, who had
two brave men so dangerously wounded that they died

---

[1] He had just succeeded the Marshal of Chaumont as grand-
master of France.

a few days afterwards at Ferrara. One was the Lord of
l'Espi, grand-master of the artillery, who had an arquebus wound in the arm, the other the Lord of Châtillon-
Coligny, provost of Paris, who received a similar wound
in the thigh. They were both men worthy of regret.

When the breach was made in the town, all those who
were ordered to give the assault approached it, to the
number of 300 men-at-arms, and 3000 foot-soldiers. The
rest of the army was arranged in as good battle order as
it could possibly be, and all showed so much desire to
fight that it seemed as if they were going to a fête. They
remained under arms for three or four hours to support
the assailants, who had enough to do; for if their attack
was good, the defence was equally so. The Viscount
d'Etoge,[2] lieutenant of the Count Robert de la Marck, and
Frederic, Count of Bozzolo, of the house of Gonzagua,
signalized themselves, and were several times thrown
from the top of the foss to the bottom. Mark Antony
Colonna, who commanded in the square, encouraged the
besieged. "Keep a good heart," said he, "I promise
you that we shall have assistance by to-morrow. The
breach is small and easy to defend, and if we let ourselves be captured, we are all lost and dishonoured."

When the French had given five or six assaults, seeing
that the breach was so well defended that they could not
enter, they beat a retreat; and this was perhaps fortunate,
for if they had entered, they would doubtless have
amused themselves with the plunder, which would have
been immense, and there might possibly have been, as

---

[2] He was of an illustrious house, since known under the names
of Boulemont and Givry. His grandson, René d'Anglere, Viscount d'Etoge, served under Henry IV. in the battles of Senlis
and d'Ivry, and at the sieges of Paris and Rouen He was
killed at the siege of Laon in 1594.

at Brescia, a great desertion, which would have caused the loss of the battle, which was given on Easter-day, the 11th of April. The Duke of Nemours withdrew his army also, so that they might rest, and be in a condition to fight, which would soon be inevitable, as the enemy was only two miles distant.

He provided supper for the principal officers, and after the meal he said to the good knight, "Lord Bayard, I must tell you that the Spaniards fear you. Our prisoners tell us that they are always asking if you are in our camp. I am of opinion that you should go yourself to-morrow morning, and so carry the news of your own arrival, and have some good skirmishing with them, which will oblige them to prepare for battle, and you will have an opportunity of judging of their appearance."

Bayard, who had never desired anything more in his life, seized the proposition, and answered, "I promise you, my lord, that before mid-day to-morrow I will have seen them so near that I shall be able to give you a good account of them."

Amongst the captains who were present was the Baron of Bearn, lieutenant of the Duke of Nemours, a brave soldier, and one who was always ready for a skirmish. He was jealous that Bayard was before him, and determined to be out before him in the morning. He confided his design to his most intimate friends, who promised to accompany him, and kept their word. We shall see how they came out of it.

Bayard returned home, and sent for his nephew, Pierrepont, who was his lieutenant, with his ensign, his standard-bearer, and several others of his company, and informed them of what he had promised the duke. He consulted them as to the manner of carrying it out, and added that his design was to unfurl for the first time the banners of the Duke of Lorraine. "I hope," said he, "that they will bring us good luck, and that they will be more beautiful than the cornets." Then he gave out his orders. He charged the bastard Du Fay, his standard-bearer, to take fifty archers, with which he was to pass the canal below the artillery of the Spaniards, and give the alarm in their camp as far as he could in safety, and to retire in good order, without hazarding anything, when he thought fit, until he met Pierrepont, who would follow him closely with thirty men-at-arms, and the rest archers; "and," added he, "if you find yourselves pressed, I shall be there to sustain you, and, believe me, if we bear ourselves bravely, we shall gain honour." The men he spoke to were too skilled not to understand his plan immediately, and they had men under their orders who were capable of commanding armies themselves. All retired to rest until the trumpet should wake them, which it did not fail to do at break of day. All were soon on foot, and in marching order. The Duke of Lorraine's banners were unfurled, and gave good courage to all the company, which was distributed, as had been arranged the evening before, in three bands, each at a bow-shot from the other.

Bayard still knew nothing of the expedition of the Baron of Bearn, who had preceded him, and who had given such a hot alarm to their enemies that all were already under arms. All went well for him up to that time; but they fired two or three cannon shots from the Spanish side, one of which carried off the arms of one of his comrades, named Bazillac, and another killed the Lord of Berzar's horse under him. Both of these gentlemen belonged to the Duke of Nemours' company. The duke was much grieved for them, especially for Bazillac, to whom he was much attached. After these artillery shots, the skirmishers were assailed by 120 Spanish and Neapolitan men-at-arms, who made them retreat, and afterwards gained the plain at full gallop. The first of the routed troop met Du Fay, who did not venture farther, and informed Bayard of the encounter. The knight sent him to join the Captain Pierrepont, and himself reached them with his troop, making of the three companies but one. Then he saw the Baron of Bearn and his flying soldiers, and the enemy following them closely, and already past the canal. He would not have taken the whole world as a gift to have changed places with any one.

"Follow me, my companions!" he cried, both to his own men and to the fugitives, "they are ours!" His voice alone rallied them, but to show them an example, he threw himself, first of all, into the midst of the Spaniards, and, soon followed by his troop, showed himself, as he always did, great in valour. His first strokes upset five or six of the enemy, who made no wonderment at that, but put themselves in good order of defence; yet at the same time they turned their backs, and crossed the canal quicker than they had come. Bayard and his soldiers pursued them quite into their camp, where all was in battle order, and where they overturned all who opposed them, and knocked down all the tents and pavilions they came to.

However, the knight, whose eye was everywhere, perceived a body of cavalry, consisting of nearly 300 men-at-arms, marching towards them in a close squadron, in order to surround them. He immediately beat a retreat, saying to Pierrepont, "There are too many men here for our small number to compete with."

They took the road to the canal, and thence returned

to their camp, without having lost a single man. The Spaniards let them go, excepting five or six, who followed them, demanding to break lances with them. Bayard would not allow it, although many of his company had a great desire to do so; but he feared that that might engage them in some new skirmish, and that the time was not propitious for such an occurrence. From the record we have of Bayard's actions, we find that his valour was always tempered with wisdom, and that, as he was the bravest officer of his age, he was also the most prudent, and his prudence never left him, even in the hottest fields.

The Duke of Nemours, informed of the knight's expedition before he arrived at the camp, ran to embrace him, saying, "You are the man, Lord Bayard, for skirmishes. No one knows so well as you do, either how to begin or how to finish them; you are our master in the art of war, as you have clearly shown to-day."

That same day, which was the eve of the battle of Ravenna, the duke assembled together all his captains, both of foot and horse, and spoke to them thus:—"You see, sirs, that we are here in a country where everything is wanting to us; and that the longer we remain here, the more exhausted we shall become. The town of Ravenna bounds us on the one side, and our enemies on the other, within cannon-shot of us. I am informed that the Venetians and Swiss threaten to descend upon the duchy of Milan, where you know we have not left strong forces. My uncle, the king, is daily pressing me to give battle, and I think, if he knew our situation, he would urge me to it still more forcibly. Thus, considering all things, I think we cannot defer it any longer; and I hope that, with the help of God and the good-will of our army, we shall, for our master's honour and our own, soon march upon our enemies. If God favours us, to Him we will render thanks; if we are unsuccessful, His will be done. As to me, do not doubt that I would sooner die than lose the day, and if God orders it so, our enemies will be cowards if they spare me, for I will not spare them. Give me your opinions now, and I will follow them." Chabannes spoke first, and voted for battle, and the sooner the better. He was supported by the grand equerry,[3] the grand seneschal of Normandy, the Lord of Crussol, Louis d'Ars, and all the other heads of the army. Battle was then fixed for the next day, Easter Sunday.

---

[3] Peter d'Urfe, grand-bailie of Forey, of an ancient and noble house now extinct.

CHAPTER XIX.

HEY began by building a bridge over the canal, of which we have spoken, for the artillery and foot-soldiers to cross by; as for the cavalry, they would have no difficulty, as the canal was fordable and the banks easy to climb. Bayard was of opinion that they should settle the plan of the battle, so that each one should know his place, and what he had to do "Because," said he, "all the prisoners whom I have questioned have told me that it is the custom of the Spaniards to make one troop of their infantry and two of their cavalry; so I think we ought to arrange our plans, taking that fact into consideration."

His advice was received with applause, and the plan was immediately arranged.

It was decreed that the lansquenets, with the foot-soldiers of Captains Molard, Bonnet, Maugiron, the Baron of Grammont, Bardassan, and others, to the number of 6000 men, should march together, and form one large body, flanked by the 2000 Gascons of Captain Odet d'Aydie, and the cadet of Duras; that all should go and place themselves at a cannon-shot from the enemy, having the artillery before them; and that they should cannonade the Spaniards to make them leave their fort, as their principal precaution had been to encamp themselves well ; that after the foot-soldiers, and quite near to them, the Duke of Ferrara and Chabannes should be placed at the head of the vanguard, and with them the gentlemen to the number of 800 men-at-arms, under the orders of the grand seneschal, the grand equerry, Humbercourt, La Cropte-Daillon, Theodore Trivulce, and others ; and finally, near them, and directly opposite, the Duke of Nemours with his company, his cousin Lautrec, D'Alègre, Louis d'Ars, Bayard, and some others, making in all 400 men-at-arms; that the Italian infantry, to the number of about 4000, should remain on the near side of the canal in care of the baggages, for fear that those of Ravenna should come and make a sally. This infantry was under the command of Counts Nicholas and Francis Scottie, of Plaisance, of the Marquis Malaspina, and other officers of the same nation. It was decided that the bastard Du Fay, having a command and with the chief standard, should guard the bridge till further orders.

As soon as the day dawned the lansquenets crossed the first ; but Captain Molard, jealous of the honour of preceding them, cried out to his men, " What ! my friends, shall it be said that the lansquenets have seen the enemy before us ? I would sooner lose one of my eyes than that should happen."

He immediately plunged into the water, and followed by all his men, up to their waists in water, they crossed the canal fully equipped, and reached the other side before the lansquenets ; the artillery crossed next, and were placed at the head of the foot-soldiers ranged in battle order ; after them the infantry passed with the men-at-arms.

During this march a singular circumstance happened. The Duke of Nemours, armed at all points, and magnificently attired in a dress blazoned with the arms of Foix and Navarre, having gone out very early in the morning, remarked that the sun rose as red as blood; he pointed it out to those who accompanied him, amongst whom was a gentleman very familiar with him, named Hautbourdin, a wit, who said to him, "Do you know, my lord, what sign that is? That is a token that some great prince or captain will die to-day: it must be either you or the Viceroy of Naples."

The duke smiled at this, as he always did at Hautbourdin's sallies; afterwards he went forward to see his army defile, which it did with great diligence. Bayard, who was near him, asked him to walk with him along the canal with the Lords of Lautrec, D'Alègre, and some others, to the number of about twenty. They saw afar off the movements of the Spanish camp, where they were preparing for battle, judging that it must take place on that day. The duke then said to Bayard, "We are just under their fire; if they had arquebusiers placed there, they could pick us off easily."

At this moment they perceived a body of twenty or thirty Spanish knights, amongst whom was the general of the cavalry, Don Pedro de Paes. Bayard advanced towards them, saluted them, and said to them, "My lords, you are walking about, as we are, waiting for the beginning of the battle; I pray you not to allow arquebuses to be fired from your side, and I promise you none shall be from ours."

This they agreed to, and then Don Pedro begged him to say who he was, the Spaniard having heard of the glory which he had acquired in the kingdom of Naples. Learning his name, he said to him with a very good grace,

"Lord Bayard, although your arrival in the French camp may not be a subject of rejoicing to us—in fact, on the contrary, we consider it as good as a reinforcement of 2000 men for them—still I am no less glad to see you; and if it please God that peace shall be established between our nations, I will prove to you the esteem I feel for you, and the wish I have to be numbered amongst your friends."

The knight returned his civility with his accustomed modesty, after which Don Pedro asked him who that lord was so magnificently accoutred, and to whom everybody paid so much respect.

"He is," said Bayard, "our general, the Duke of Nemours, the brother of your queen."

He had hardly spoken, when this Spaniard and all with him advanced towards the duke, dismounted and did homage to him, assuring him that, saving the service of the king their master, they would profess themselves his servants all their lives. The duke received their compliment very graciously, and after a little conversation they separated, each to his post.

The French, while marching, perceived the enemy's vanguard, commanded by Fabricius Colonna, full in sight, and within gun-shot distance. Bayard and D'Alègre remarked the circumstance to the Duke of Nemours.

"Do you see," said he, "that magnificent troop of horsemen? If we only had two pieces of artillery here, we could easily reach them."

D'Alègre went himself to order a cannon and a culverin to be brought forward, which they fired so vigorously and so quickly on the enemy's troop that they had 300 men-at-arms down in a moment; and their chief, the Lord Fabricius, declared, when he was a prisoner at

Ferrara, that a single shot had killed thirty-three men. The Spaniards were terribly frightened, not knowing whence the shots came that overthrew them. Their general had expressly commanded them not to leave their posts until the French should go to attack them; but they were forced to leave their places, notwithstanding their commanding officer, to whom they said in their tongue, "By the body of God, we are going to fight men, and Heaven crushes us!"

However, from the side of the Spanish camp, which was extremely strong, and protected by a good ditch, the artillery had begun its play. Behind the foss all the foot-soldiers, to protect themselves from the French, were lying on their faces: their defence, which was in front of them, consisted of twenty pieces, cannons and culverins too, and about 200 arquebuses à croc, and between each two a little wheeled truck, upon which were sharp pieces of iron, like scythes, to cut down the French foot-soldiers as they advanced. On one wing was Fabricius Colonna with the vanguard, composed of 800 men-at-arms; a little higher up was the body of the army, commanded by Don Raymond of Cardonna, who had more than 400 men-at-arms; and still nearer to him were 2000 Italians, commanded by Ramassot. But as to their soldiery, never were seen finer or more active troops.

As soon as the Duke of Nemours had passed the canal, he gave orders that all should march, notwithstanding the enemies' fire, which picked out the French infantry as if they had been targets, and had already killed 2000 before the battle commenced; amongst others four captains, who were much regretted—Jarses, Le Hérisson, Molard, and Philip of Friberg, all brave men, full of courage and experience. However, notwithstanding the Spanish fire, the French did not slacken speed, but still marched forward. On the other side, the vanguard, commanded by Fabricius Colonna, driven out, as we have seen, came into the open field to fight, and marched straight to the point where the Duke of Nemours and some few of the soldiery were.

The French in this body, overjoyed at commencing the attack, rushed upon their enemies. The Spaniards had divided into two parties, thinking to surround their opponents. Bayard saw it at first, and advised the duke to divide his men into two bodies, which was immediately done. Then the Spaniards began crying with all their might, "Spain!" "St. Iago, à os cavallos!" (upon the horses), and fell upon the French, only wishing to kill their horses; but they were received with equal fury by the French, who cried, "France!" "France!" "To horse!" and, like their enemies, tried to unhorse them, according to the proverb, which says, "Kill the horse, and the man-at-arms is lost." There was never, perhaps, a more bloody and furious combat than that which was fought then, and which lasted more than an hour and a-half. Both parties were obliged to stop and take breath; then they began their ordinary cries more briskly than before. The Spaniards were half as numerous again as the French.[1]

The Lord D'Alègre, seeing the victory undecided, ran to the vanguard, and cried to the band of the Lord of la Marck, whom he met the first, and who was distinguishable by his black and white colours, "*After me, black and white and the archers of the guard!*"

---

[1] The Spanish army consisted of 20,000 men, and the French of 15,400, according to an account kept in the record chamber at Grenoble; but we see that 4,000 remained to guard the baggage.

The Duke of Ferrara and Chabannes, concluding that pressing necessity had induced him to call them, sent their men at full speed towards the Duke of Nemours, who had already made the enemy retreat by degrees. This reinforcement was fatal to the Spanish, for these archers of the guard carried on their saddle-bows, little hatchets, which were useful to them in putting up their tents: they used them now, and gave the Spaniards such terrific blows with them that they knocked down every man they touched. Finally, they forced the enemy to leave the camp, leaving 300 or 400 men-at-arms on the field between the two ditches, besides many Neapolitan lords whom they took prisoners, and whose lives were saved.

Bayard, seeing the Duke of Nemours covered with blood, and with the brains of one of his slain men by his side, asked him if he were not wounded, as he thought he was.

"No," said the duke, "but I have wounded others."

"God be praised," Bayard replied, "the battle is yours. You have covered yourself with glory to-day; but remain here, assemble your soldiers, and do not allow them to begin plundering. It is not time for that yet. The Captain Louis d'Ars and I are going to follow the fugitives, and hinder them from leaving before their foot-soldiers; but do not leave here till he or I come to you." The duke promised to do as Bayard wished, but did not keep his word, and paid for it by his life in a manner which deserves a detailed account.

We have noticed that, at the commencement of the action, the Spanish foot-soldiers had thrown themselves flat on their faces to escape the fire of the French artillery, and that their fort was so constructed that they could not be seen, so that it was very dangerous to attack them. Now the French were only two pikes' length from them. The 2000 Gascons were then ordered to go, in spite of the danger, and attack them from the rear, and discharge their arrows at them to make them get up. The Captain Odet and the Captain Duras got ready to do so; but they explained that they wanted some pikemen to support them, in case their foot-soldiers, having discharged all their arrows, should be charged by Spanish ensigns. The Lord of Moncaure was ordered to go and help them with 1000 Picards whom he commanded.

The archers discharged their arrows, and slew a great number of Spaniards, which obliged the others to rise, and form in battle order: but two ensigns immediately appeared behind them, with 1000 or 1200 men each, who fell upon the Gascons, and broke them (whether it was their fault or that of the Picards), killed the Lord of Moncaure, the lieutenant of the Captain Odet, that of the cadet of Duras, and many other very good officers. The Spanish uttered loud cries of joy, as if they had gained the battle, although their defeat was already decided, and the two ensigns returned no more to their rear, but took the road to Ravenna, marching four abreast along the bank of the canal. We must leave them a moment, and relate what followed the attack of the Gascons. The Spanish, standing, advanced upon the border of their ditch, where, the French assailed them with incredible bravery; but they were received with arquebus strokes, which killed many of them; amongst others, that famous Captain Jacob, whom we have before mentioned with honour; he received a gun-shot through the body, which only gave him time to say to his comrades in his own tongue, "Friends, serve the king as well as he serves us," and he immediately fell dead. He had brought with him a captain named Fabian, one of the largest, handsomest, and strongest men that could be seen, who, seeing his good friend and commander slain, only wished to live to avenge his death, and performed a deed of unexampled strength and bravery. He threw himself into the middle of the Spaniards' pikes, holding his own across, and made them lower their points to the earth, where he held them by the strength of his arms alone, and by that means gave the French an opportunity of leaping the ditch, which was not accomplished without much bloodshed on both sides, for a better defence was never seen than that which the Spaniards opposed to this attack.

The French lost in this action the Baron of Grammont, the Lords of Maugiron and Bardassan, who had been prodigiously valorous. The Captain Bonnet received a pike-thrust in the forehead, and the head remained in the wound. In fine, the loss of the French was great, not only in number, but considering also the quality and merit of the dead; but on the Spanish side it was very different, for whilst they supported the attack from the ditch of which we have spoken, the soldiers of the French vanguard, having attacked them on the flank, routed them, and did not leave one of them, excepting only the general, Don Pedro of Navarre,[2] and some other principal officers, whom they took prisoners.

To return to those two ensigns whom we have seen taking the road to Ravenna, and following the course

---

[2] He was a soldier of fortune. His merit and talents promoted him to the first military dignities. It is said that he was the first to invent mines. He passed from the Spanish service to that of France, under Francis I.

of the canal. The Duke of Nemours remaining at the place where Bayard had urgently recommended him to await news of the action, perceived these two ensigns, who were retiring, whilst some of the defeated Gascons were flying towards him. He asked what it was. One of the fugitives replied, " The Spaniards have defeated us."

The prince, thinking that his whole infantry was routed, without looking to see whether he was accompanied or not, rushed to their rescue in despair into that way, having only fourteen or fifteen men with him.

To complete the misfortune, the Spaniards had reloaded several arquebuses, which they fired on him and his escort, then fell upon them with their pikes. The French could not easily move, not only because the road was narrow, but it was bordered on one side by a canal, and on the other by a very deep ditch. All the escort was killed or thrown into the canal or ditch. The duke's horse having been hamstrung, his loss compelled his master to fight on foot, having no other defensive weapon than his sword. Assailed by a crowd of enemies, he defended himself like a true hero. He was vigorously seconded by his cousin Lautrec, who cried to the Spanish, " Do not kill him; he is our general, the brother of your queen."

In spite of Lautrec's cries, they finished him, having given him so many cuts that he had fourteen or fifteen on his face alone. Vivarotz, son of the Lord d'Alègre, was thrown into the ditch, and his father had already been killed at the defeat of the foot-soldiers. Lautrec and some others were left for dead, after which the Spanish fled along the same road, which was nearly ten miles long.

Half way, they met Bayard returning from the pur-

suit of the fugitives, with about forty men, so fatigued
that neither they nor their horses could keep up. However, they considered it their duty to charge them, and
prepared to do so; but one of the Spanish chiefs advanced from the ranks, and said to him, "What do you
want to do? You must plainly see that you have not
enough men with you to fight against us. You have
gained the battle, in which all our men have lost their
lives, and it is only by a miracle that we have escaped.
Be satisfied with the honour of the victory, and let us
pass."

Bayard consented to this, on condition that they
should give up the ensigns. They gave them up, and
then gave the knight a passage through the middle
of their troop, and continued their road. Alas! if
he had known of their last exploit, and that the Duke
of Nemours had just died by their hands, he would not
have let them go without attacking them, and would
have rather died a thousand times than not have
avenged himself.

During the battle, and before the total defeat of the
Spaniards, the Viceroy, Don Raymont of Cardona,
had fled with 300 men-at-arms, and Ramassot with his
2000 Italian foot-soldiers. These were all that escaped;
the remainder were killed or taken prisoners. The battle
had commenced at eight o'clock in the morning, and it
was four in the afternoon when Bayard and the others
returned to the camp. The news of the Duke of Nemours' death was already spread there, and the consternation, cries, and tears were such that 2,000 fresh
troops would have been more than a match for the
whole army, more especially that all were spent with
fatigue. The body of the duke was carried to his
lodgings by his gentlemen, and there the crying and

sobbing began again, and did not leave off for a long time, this prince, the most accomplished man of his time, knew so well how to gain the friendship, confidence, and hearts of all his army, both great and small.

Finally, we must say of this battle of Ravenna that perhaps there never was such a cruel, murderous engagement, and that on both sides they fought with a fury that history furnishes few examples of. If the Spaniards lost many, their number being, as we have seen, nearly twice as numerous as that of the French, and nearly all being left dead on the field, we must also confess that the loss on the French side was very great, on account of the great number of good officers who perished there. Their greatest loss was that of the incomparable Duke of Nemours, in whom nature had united all human virtues, and who, if he had lived, would have been King of Naples; but God disposed of him according to His will. With him died on this unhappy day the brave D'Alègre and his son Vivarotz, La Cropte-Daillon, the Lieutenant D'Humbercourt, the Captains Molard, Jacob, De Friberg, Maugiron, the Baron of Grammont, Bardassan, and many others; about 3000 foot-soldiers, twenty-four men-at-arms under the king's orders, seven gentlemen of his house, and nine archers of his guard. The greater number of those who did not perish on this bloody day were wounded.

On the Spanish side twenty captains of infantry regiments and nearly 10,000 of their men died; of their cavalry more than thirty captains or standard-bearers, with 800 men-at-arms, besides Don Menaldo of Cardona, Don Diego of Quignonez, and the Captains Alvarado and Alphonse of Stella. Their infantry general, Don Pedro of Navarre, was made prisoner there, with

Don John of Cardona, the Marquises of Licite, of La Padule, and of Pescara, the Duke of Traijetter, the Counts of Conches and of Pepoli, the Cardinal de Médicis, the Pope's legate, and more than 100 other lords or captains. All the artillery, the arquebuses, and baggage remained there. In fine, out of an army of more than 20,000 men, 16,000 were slain or taken. The Lord Mark Antony Colonna had the good fortune to retire into the citadel of Ravenna, which was strong, and capable of a good defence.

The next day the town was plundered by the lansquenets and the French foot-soldiers, notwithstanding the defences which had been made. This was by the base orders of the Captain Jacquin Caumont, whose death verified the horoscope of the astrologer of Carpi; for Chabannes, who had been placed at the head of the army, had him hanged.

This day at Ravenna would have been great in its results had it not been for the death of the Duke of Nemours, and the French would, doubtless, have profited by their victory, but this misfortune, added to the news that the Lord Trivulce incessantly gave them, that the Venetians and the Swiss menaced the duchy of Milan; and that, on the other hand, the emperor began to bestir himself, to declare war to the king, determined them to take the road to the duchy of Milan.

CHAPTER XX.

Letter of the Knight Bayard to Laurent Alleman, his uncle, on the battle of Ravenna.

" Sir,

COMMEND myself with all humility to your good favour.

" Since I last wrote to you we have had, as you have doubtless learnt, a battle with our enemies. But, to make you acquainted with the whole affair, it happened in this way. Our army came and lodged close to this city of Ravenna; our enemies were there as soon as we, in order to give heart to the said town, and by reason of some rumours which were daily current of the descent of the Swiss, and of the want of provisions in our camp, Monsieur de Nemours resolved to give battle, and, last Sunday, passed a little river, which was between our said enemies and ourselves. Thus it fell out that we engaged them. They marched in the best order, and were more than 1700 men-at-arms, the proudest and most triumphant that we ever saw, and 14,000 foot soldiers, as gallant men as could be met with. So about 1000 of their men-at-arms, enraged at our artillery, fell upon our squadron in which was the Duke of Nemours in person; his company, that of the

Duke of Lorraine, of Louis d'Ars and others, to the number of 400 men-at-arms or thereabouts, who received their said enemies with such valour, that better fighting was never seen. Between our vanguard, which was composed of 1000 men-at-arms and us, there were great ditches, and, moreover, it had work to do elsewhere, and could not help us. So it happened that the said squadron was obliged to stand the brunt of the said 1000 men-at-arms of the enemy. Just then Monsieur de Nemours broke his lance, and pierced one of their men-at-arms through his body, and half the length of an arm beyond. So the said 1000 men-at-arms were defeated and put to flight, and as we were in pursuit of them, we met their foot-soldiers near their artillery, with 500 or 600 men-at-arms, who were there hemmed in, and had put little trucks upon two wheels before them, upon which were pieces of iron of the length of two or three arms, and they came to a hand-to-hand fight with our foot-soldiers. Their said foot-soldiers had so many arquebuses, that when they fought close in this manner, they killed all our captains, so to speak, instead of staggering them, or putting them to flight. But our soldiers were so well seconded by the men-at-arms that, after fighting well, our said enemies were defeated, lost their artillery, and 700 or 800 men-at-arms, and the greater number of their captains, with 7000 or 8000 foot-soldiers. It is not known whether any captains escaped, but the viceroy, for we have taken prisoner the Lord Fabricius Colonna, the Cardinal de Médicis, the Pope's legate, Pedro Navarre, the Marquis of Pescara, the Marquis of Padule, the son of the Prince of Malfi, Don, man of Cardona, son of the Marquis of Bélonde, and others whose names I do not know. Those who escaped were followed for eight or ten miles, and are now making their way across the mountains, although some say the serfs (peasants) have cut them to pieces.

"My lord, if the king has gained the battle, I swear to you that the poor gentlemen have lost it, for while we gave chase the Duke de Nemours saw some of our foot-soldiers who required help. He rushed to their rescue, but the gentle prince was so badly accompanied that he was killed. Of all grief and mourning that were ever known, never was so much sorrow, surely, as has been and is now being shown in our camp, for it almost seems as if we had lost the battle. I promise you, my lord, it is the most pitiful death of any prince these hundred years; and, if he had lived to be old, he would have done deeds that no other prince ever did before him. The soldiers well may say they have lost their father, and as for me, my lord, I cannot be cheerful, for I have lost so much that I cannot give you an idea of it in writing. On other parts of the field were killed the Lord d'Alègre, and his son, Monseigneur de Molard, six German captains, and the Captain Jacob, their colonel, the Captain Maugiron, the Baron of Grammont, and more than 200 gentlemen of good name and merit, not reckoning more than 2000 of our footmen. I assure you that the kingdom of France will not recover the loss it has sustained in 100 years.

"Yesterday morning the body of the late duke was taken to Milan with all possible honours. Two hundred men-at-arms accompanied him, and carried before him eighteen or twenty of the most triumphant banners gained in this battle. He will remain at Milan till the king has sent word if he will have him conveyed to France or not. My lord, our army is going temporarily by the Romagna, taking all the towns for the council of Pisa. They will not wait for us to implore them to give themselves up, they will be afraid of being plundered as Ravenna has been, in which nothing remains. And we shall not stir from that quarter till the king has sent word what he wishes his army to do.

"When this is despatched, I think we shall have abstinence from war. The Swiss are always making a noise somewhere; but when they know of this defeat perhaps they will put a little water in their wine. As soon as things are a little settled I shall come and see you. Praying God, my lord, to give you a happy and long life. Written at the camp of Ravenna, this 14th day of April.

"Your very humble servant,

"BAYARD."

CHAPTER XXI.

HEN all the army had arrived in the duchy of Milan, they began by paying the last honours to the Duke of Nemours. His obsequies were conducted with more pomp and ceremony than are ordinarily displayed at the funerals of kings. More than 10,000 men in mourning attended the corpse, the greater number on horseback, four flags taken from the enemy preceded his coffin, drooping to the earth. Afterwards came his ensigns, and his standard-bearer, and he was placed in the church of the Duomo, which is the Cathedral, honoured with the tears and regrets of all present. The captains being assembled after the ceremony was over, the command was transferred to the Lord of La Palisse, Jacques de Chabannes, as the oldest man, and the one most worthy of this honour, because the Lord of Lautrec, dangerously wounded, had been taken to Ferrara, where the duke and duchess gave him all the care they could, and had the satisfaction of seeing him recover his health.

The Pope Julius the Second, always an open enemy to France, was not satisfied, because he had not been able to make the emperor declare against the king. He had persuaded him to order his lansquenets, the few that were left from the battle of Ravenna, to return. His orders, addressed to their commander, brother of the dead Captain Jacob, were so precise, that he considered it necessary to obey, and the greater number left the French army, where only 700 or 800 remained, who were retained by a young captain, who, having nothing to lose in Germany, attached himself to the service of the king.

The Cardinal de Médicis, made prisoner at the battle of Ravenna, was upon the point of being sent to France, where he would doubtless have been kept a long time, but he had the good fortune to be delivered by a party of the Pope's men, commanded by Matthew of Beccarea, who rendered him a great service, for if it had not been for him, he would never have borne either tiara, or the name of Leo X.

The fear that the French had for the Venetians and Swiss was found to be only too well founded, the latter came down in great numbers into the duchy of Milan, and were reinforced by the Pope's troops. The French army was too fatigued and too small to show front to them. They disputed several passages with them pretty successfully, but at last they were obliged to yield to numbers, and to retire to Pavia, where they hoped to remain. The French were only there two days when, notwithstanding the diligence they had displayed in barricading and fortifying the gates, the Swiss entered the town (it has never been discovered by what means), and gained the great square, where the alarm was soon spread. The Captain Louis d'Ars, who had been made governor, went immediately to the place, and did great things. Chabannes and Humbercourt followed him, and Bayard, of course, who surpassed himself. Amongst other doings, he stopped the Swiss with about thirty-six of his company, and kept them fighting incessantly for more than two hours, and in this time he had two horses killed under him.

It was by his advice that the French, on entering the town, had at first constructed a bridge of boats (although there was a stone one there), so that they might have a certain way of retreat in case of need. The event clearly showed the wisdom of this precaution, for as soon as the Swiss had commenced their attack, they had the artillery taken off to be carried across the bridge. While they were still at work, Captain Pierrepont, who was on the watch, came to warn the French that above their bridge fresh troops were arriving to the Swiss, on little boats, with about ten men on each; that if they chose to make one troop, they could seize the bridge, shut them in, and conquer them easily. On this warning, every one took the road to the bridge, where there were many blows given, and much blood shed on both sides.

However, the cavalry passed, and they left 300 lansquenets to guard the bridge. But this was one of those unfortunate days on which disgrace seems to succeed disgrace without remorse. As the last piece of artillery (a long culverin taken at Ravenna) was passing, it sunk the first boat, and so cut off the route from the lansquenets, who took to flight, and saved themselves as they best could; some were slain, others thrown into the Ticino, and very few escaped. When the French had all passed they broke the bridge, and thus stopped their pursuers. But the day's misfortunes were not yet complete.

Bayard, who had remained the last, according to custom, to superintend the breaking of the bridge, received a falcon-shot fired from the town, which struck his shoulder in passing, and cut off the flesh to the bone. Those who saw the blow thought it had killed him; but our hero, who was never frightened at anything, was not disconcerted, and though he felt extreme pain, he relieved his companions by telling them that his wound was nothing, as though it had in reality been a very small matter.

However, the blood flowed in such abundance, that they had a good deal of trouble to staunch it; but as there was no surgeon there, his men tore up their shirts for bandages. Others put tree-moss upon the wound. In fine they did all they could to put him in a fit state to follow the army, which retired to Alexandria, where there was a bridge, which had been made under the auspices of Theodore Trivulce, who had gone on before for that purpose. The army did not remain there long; it was soon obliged to leave Lombardy entirely, excepting the citadels of Milan, Cremona, Lugano, and Lucerne, and some places in the Valentine, with the town and castle of Brescia.

This army, or rather this remnant, repassed the Alps, and lodged in different garrisons. Bayard, though still suffering from his wound, followed it, and went to Grenoble, to the bishop, his uncle, who had never seen him since he left him in the hands of the Duke of Savoy as his page.

It is needless to tell with what demonstrations of joy he was received, and the good bishop's satisfaction at the warlike renown he had acquired in the long interval of twenty-two years since they met.

He received many testimonies of esteem and admiration on the part of the nobility. Each outvied the other in giving him fêtes; and all, even the ladies, congratulated themselves on the honour his presence did to their province. He could not have been in a better place for the recovery of his health; but whether on account of an issue from his last wound, or from the great fatigues he had borne in many succeeding campaigns, he was attacked with a violent fever which lasted seventeen days, and brought him very low indeed. When he found himself in this state, his regret was not that death was near, but that he must die in his bed.

"Oh, heaven!" he cried, "if it was your will to take me to yourself, why did you not let me die at the feet of that matchless Duke of Nemours, with my brave companions! Why did I not die when I was so grievously wounded at the assault of Brescia! I should have accepted death with joy, following the example of all my ancestors who have died on the field of battle. I have been so many times exposed there, I have braved so much, and on so many perilous occasions, in assaults or skirmishes, and have I only escaped to come here and die in a bed like a woman. But, God, Thy will be done. All my confidence is in Thy mercy, I am a great sinner, but I hope Thou wilt pardon my faults, and accept the sacrifice of my life, as an expiation for them." His regrets and sentiments of piety were so touching, that all the attendants were bathed in tears.

While he was in this state, all in the town, both great and small, nobles and common people, the bishop and the clergy, and even the nuns, prayed incessantly for Bayard's preservation. At last God was favourable to their prayers, his fever decreased by degrees, and in eight or ten days left him entirely.

His recovery was slow, but with time, and the care they took of him, his health was entirely re-established, and during the few months that he continued at Grenoble, he gave fêtes to the ladies, and was fêted by them in return.

During this interval, there happened to our hero a gallant adventure which I shall relate with pleasure, because Bayard happily escaped therefrom, and, in some measure, imitated the continence of Scipio.

His valet-de-chambre, having one day discovered a young and beautiful girl, whose mother, the widow of a man of gentle blood, was so poor, that she often wanted bread both for herself and child, brought this girl, persuaded more by force than will, secretly to Bayard's cabinet, where they awaited his return.

When he arrived, the roguish valet told him that he had made one of the finest discoveries in the world, and that he had with him, for his amusement, at that moment, a young lady, who was not only beautiful, but noble.

At the same time he showed her to Bayard, who beheld a creature beautiful as an angel, but with her eyes inflamed with the tears that she had shed, and still continued to pour forth.

"What is the matter, my beautiful child?" said the knight, "why do you weep so bitterly?"

"Alas," cried she, throwing herself at his knees, "I know too well that my mother has delivered me to your will; but I assure you that I am a virgin, that my honour has never been sullied, and I would rather that I were dead than behold myself in your hands, for my mother has only brought me here through her own and my misery, for we shall die with hunger."

Then again her sobs broke forth with redoubled vigour, and Bayard, moved almost to tears, seeing so much virtue in this young creature, said to her: "In truth, my dear young lady, I am very far from seeking to overthrow those noble thoughts which I find in you.

I have always respected virtue, more so when it is accompanied by birth. Pray recover yourself, and come with me, and I will place you in a house where your honour shall be in safety."

So saying, he took a torch from his valet, and he himself conducted the young lady to the house of a relative who lived near.

On the morning of the next day he sent for the mother, whom he deeply reproached for dishonouring herself and daughter in the manner I have related; "especially," said he, "being of a noble race, you are still more criminal." The poor woman, thoroughly frightened, assured him that her daughter was pure, and that want and misery were the only causes of her crime.

"But tell me," said Bayard, "has no one yet asked her in marriage of you?"

"One of our neighbours," she replied, "an honest and well-to-do man spoke to me about her a short time since, but he wants 600 florins with her, and all I possess in the world is not worth half the money."

"And would he marry her," replied Bayard, "if she had this sum?"

"Yes, my lord, certainly he would," answered the widow.

Then the knight ordered a purse to be brought from which he took 300 crowns, saying: "Here are 200 crowns, which are worth a little more than 600 florins, to marry your daughter, and 100 crowns to buy her dresses. Moreover, he gave her 100 crowns more for herself, and ordered his valet to watch the mother and daughter, and to give him an account of them till the marriage was contracted, which took place three days after. The generosity of Bayard was rewarded by the satisfaction he felt in having preserved the honour of a noble and virtuous girl, and by his generosity having made a woman exemplary and respectable.

After he had passed some time in Dauphiny, fêted and caressed by everybody, the king, Louis XII, sent an army into Guienne, under the orders of the Duke of Longueville, to recover the kingdom of Navarre from Ferdinand, King of Arragon, who had a short time before usurped it from the King John d'Albret, to whom it belonged in right of his wife Catharine de Foix. This enterprise was not successful; the army having been a long time in the country without any success, a part commanded by Chabannes was forced to recross the Pyrenees, with the King of Navarre. A little while after they were followed by Bayard, leading a number of heavy pieces of artillery, with a detachment of soldiers, who, on the road, took some little fortresses, and finally came to lay siege to Pampeluna.

At four leagues from this town was a castle, whose taking became interesting in detail, not because it was very strong in itself, but because it could contain enough men to succour the town, or at least to make the besiegers uneasy. The King of Navarre and Chabannes begged Bayard to accept the charge of making himself master of it. He accepted the commission in the spirit of a man who had never found any difficulty in anything. He took with him his company, who were as well disposed for war as he was, and composed of men, who had most of them, as we have already said, commanded themselves. He there joined the company of Captain Bonneval, another excellent officer, many adventurers, and about 800 lansquenets, and went in open day straight to the castle. He began by sending a trumpet to summon those who were there to give it back to the King of Navarre, to whom it belonged, assuring them that their lives and baggage should be saved, but if they were taken by assault, no quarter should be shown to anyone.

Those within the castle were all good soldiers, 100 Spaniards, very loyal to their king, and they had been put there by the Duke of Naxara and the Alcalde of Donzelles,[1] both of whom Ferdinand had appointed, the one viceroy, the other lieutenant-general in the kingdom of Navarre. Their answer was that they would keep the place, and not give it up, still less would they submit personally. As soon as this answer had been reported to Bayard, he had a battery constructed, furnished with four large pieces of cannon, and beat a breach without delay. The besieged, on their side, had a good number of arquebuses with two falconets, and answered very well to the French artillery; but notwithstanding all this, in less than an hour, the breach was large enough, although difficult of access, because it was necessary to get up to it. Then Bayard sounded to the assault, and commanded the lansquenets to march and do their duty; but it was necessary, before arranging them, to come to terms with them; they told him, through their interpreter, that, according to their treaty, when a place was taken by assault they should receive double pay; that if this demand were acceded to, they would go cheerfully to the breach, otherwise not. Bayard was ignorant of this treaty; however he promised them that if they took this place by assault their demands should be satisfied. But they undoubtedly expected to be paid in advance, for not one

---

[1] Don Didago Ferdinand, of Cardoue, one of the bravest and best officers of his time.

moved from his place. The adventurers alone marched boldly, and found work to do, for, if they knew how to attack, those within knew equally well how to defend themselves.

Bayard, seeing that three attacks had been unsuccessful, had had retreat sounded, and afterwards caused cannons to be fired, apparently to enlarge the breach, but really to throw the besieged off the track, for there had entered his mind one of those expedients which were never wanting to him when occasion required. To put it in execution, he addressed himself to one of the men-at-arms, whose bravery and good conduct he knew, named La Vergne, and said to him : " Companion, will you do a bold deed, for which I will richly reward you ? Do you see that large tower which forms the corner of the rear of the castle? I want you to take with you thirty or forty brave men, and whilst I give the assault, and occupy the enemy at the breach, you shall lead your men, supplied with ladders, to enter it there. I am sure you will find no one, and you know what you have to do."

La Vergne was a man skilled in the art of war, and it was not necessary to say any more to him. He understood the plan, and executed it to perfection, while Bayard had the assault given with more impetuosity than the first time. The besieged were all at the breach, and were strangely surprised to hear behind them the cry of "France! France! Navarre! Navarre!" And to see themselves charged from the back by La Vergne and his fifty men. They wished, however, to defend themselves, but at that instant the besiegers entered by the breach, which they knocked all to pieces or very nearly so, and then plundered the place. Bayard left a small garrison there under the charge of a gentleman belonging to the King of Navarre, and as he was preparing to set out to rejoin the French camp, the lansquenets who had refused to serve, and who had done nothing, had the impudence to ask him, through their interpreter, for the double pay which he had promised them. The proposition irritated him. "Tell those rascally lansquenets," he replied, "that I would sooner give each a halter to hang himself with. The cowards wouldn't go to the breach, and now they ask double pay. I will inform the Duke of Suffolk, their commander, of it, and the Lord of Chabannes, that he may get rid of them; they are worth nothing." Their interpreter, having returned them this answer, they began to murmur loudly, like men just ready to revolt. But Bayard sounded to the standard, and assembled his adventurers, and his men-at-arms, resolved to exterminate them to the last man, if they made the least movement. They chose the better part, which was to be quiet, and return with the others to the camp at Pampeluna.

This adventure, instead of ending in a bloody manner, as it might have done, terminated by a comic scene with which the reader will be amused.

When Bayard returned from this expedition, he was received by the King of Navarre, Chabannes, the Duke of Suffolk, and the other captains, with all the expressions of satisfaction that his skill and the service he had just rendered merited. He related to them the insolent pretention of the lansquenets, and told them what had happened, at which they only laughed. In the evening he gave a supper to the Duke of Suffolk, and to many other officers of the first rank. The supper was abundant and delicate, and all were merry, when, at the end of the meal, Pierrepont came to tell Bayard that there was a tipsy lansquenet who was looking for him to kill him. The knight left the table, laughing, took his sword in his hand, and addressing himself to the lansquenet: "Comrade," said he, "are you the man that is looking for Captain Bayard, to kill him? I am he; defend yourself."

The tipsy fellow was terribly afraid, and replied, trembling, and jabbering bad French: "It is not I alone who wish to kill you, but all the lansquenets together."

"Mercy," cried Bayard, "all the lansquenets! Quarter, my comrade, I don't feel capable of fighting 6000 or 7000 men."

All the company laughed at the adventure, and Bayard, for their amusement, made the lansquenet come in. He placed him at table opposite himself, and supplied him with such frequent and copious bumpers, that he finished by leaving him as tipsy as he found him, and then sent him away. The lansquenet, well satisfied, swore to Bayard that he would be his friend for life, that he was a worthy man, that his wine was good, and that he would defend him against all the lansquenets in the world. This scene lasted a considerable time, and diverted all the company, who laughed till they cried at the conversation that the wine caused this man to indulge in, and which his bad French made still more amusing.

But to return to the siege of Pampeluna. The day after the re-entrance of Bayard into the camp, the place was breached, and they tried to give the assault there, but the alcalde of Los Donzelles, who was shut up there, defended it so well, that the French were obliged to suspend the assault, after having lost many men there. The result of this campaign was very unfortunate. The army, on entering Navarre, had made there a general waste of all the good things of the earth;

the corn magazines had been blown up, and the millstones broken; they soon had reason to repent of this, for everything was wanting at once, and the famine became so great, that many soldiers died of it; added to that, the troops were barefooted, and ragged, so that they were full of misfortunes.

In this sad plight, and to finish their disgrace, they learnt that the Duke of Naxara was advancing with a body of from 8000 to 10,000 men, and that he was already at the Pont-de-la-Reine. All these circumstances caused Chabannes, and all the officers, to advise the King of Navarre to put off the expedition to another time, in consequence of which the siege was removed in broad daylight, and the artillery taken away; but it did not go far, for they had hardly gone two or three days' journey with it, with almost incredible trouble and expense, by a hilly road, when they had to leave it, and shatter it to pieces, so that the enemy should not profit by it. Added to this, they were continually harassed in their retreat, and had bloody skirmishes to withstand.

CHAPTER XXII.

THE Duke of Suffolk was in this army, and had formed a very close friendship with our hero.

One day after a vigorous skirmish, which lasted till the evening, he retired; overcome with lassitude, hunger, and thirst, he came to beg some supper of Bayard, "For," he said, "I have not broken my fast, and my men have told me that there is nothing to eat at my house."

"Very willingly," replied Bayard, "I will entertain you well."

Then calling his butler, he ordered him to hasten the supper, and, added he, "Let us be served as well as if we were in Paris." Suffolk laughed with all his heart at this joke, knowing that no one in the army had had anything but millet bread for two days; but he was agreeably surprised at being regaled as if he had indeed been in Paris.

The French retired, with the enemy in pursuit, which disturbed them much. However, the retreat was not so unfortunate as it might have been. Bayard especially acquired much honour, being always in the rear-guard, and turning and facing the enemy, whom he often made repent of their rashness. In fine, the army reached

Bayonne, where it found plenty to make up for the previous famine; but this abundance even was a misfortune, for many soldiers died from over-eating.

This year, 1512, closed with three events. Firstly, the Venetians returned to favour, and made peace with the king. Secondly, the pope, Julius II., the irreconcilable enemy of the king and the French nation, died. He had always either been fighting against them, or quarrelling with them, as we have seen in the course of this history, and he carried his hatred and ill-will to the grave. He was succeeded by the Cardinal de Médicis, the same who was made prisoner at the battle of Ravenna, who took the title of Leo X. He was a very wise man, protector, or rather restorer of the sciences, very ambitious, and a great politician. The third event was, that the English made a descent upon Brittany, in which they were not successful. One day one of their largest vessels fought against one of the ships of Queen Anne, Duchess of Brittany. The English ship, named the Regent, carried the most brilliant nobility of the kingdom, and in large numbers. It ran against the queen's ship, named the Franciscan nun, but as during the combat they threw fire into each other, they were both burnt, and not one on board escaped.

The year 1513 began by an expedition into Italy, whence the French were again obliged to retire with great loss. The army, commanded by the illustrious Louis de la Trimouille, lost a battle against the Swiss near Novarra, in which many were killed on both sides. Two sons of the Lord of La Marck were left there for dead. Their father, in despair at this misfortune, went there with his company of 100 men-at-arms, to see them again, or perish with them. He made such a furious charge that he drove back the conquerors to a ditch, where his two sons lay amongst the dead. He put one across his horse before him, and a servant took the other in the same manner, and thus they took them to the camp, pierced through and through with wounds. However, they recovered in time. The elder was afterwards the Marshal of Fleurange, and the other the Lord of Jametry, and both became very illustrious men.[1]

After this said expedition into Italy, and when the army was in France after its return, the king was not long idle. Henry VIII., king of England, at the instigation of the pope, and of Ferdinand, king of Arragon, and through information received from the Emperor Maximilian I., made a raid in Picardy, near Calais, with powerful forces. Louis sent proportionate forces against him, under the orders of Louis of Hawin, Lord of Fiennes, governor of the province, and with him Bayard and a number of other good captains.

The English had no sooner disembarked than they went straight to lay siege to Terouana, which was a good place, and well fortified. It was defended by two brave men, the seneschal of Rouergue, Francis of

---

[1] History has a singular story of the battle of Novarra. The evening before it was given all the dogs in the French army, after howling for a considerable time, suddenly crossed in a pack to the Swiss camp, as if they had known that they were soon to change masters. This is not the only historical case we have of such conduct on the part of dogs. It is related in English history that Richard II. had a beautiful greyhound who had never caressed any but him. This prince, having been defeated and made prisoner by the Duke of Lancaster, who disputed his right to the crown, the hound crossed over to him, and overwhelmed him with caresses. The duke was much surprised, and asked Richard what it meant. Richard replied, " It is a good omen for you. This dog knows no other master but the king of England. I was king yesterday, you are king to-day."

Téligny, and Antony of Créqui, Lord of Pontdomi.
They had under their command their companies of
men-at-arms, a good number of adventurers, and a
body of lansquenets, commanded by their captain
Brandec. There were enough to defend the place well,
if they had had sufficient provisions and munition ; but,
says a contemporary historian, those were nearly always
the causes that prevented success.

The English army was commanded by the Duke of
Suffolk (Charles Brandon) and the Captain Talbot.
Whilst they cannonaded the place, the king of England
disembarked, and he was nearly taken prisoner on the
road from Calais to Terouana. He had with him nearly
12,000 foot-soldiers, amongst whom were 4000 lansquenets, but not a single horse-soldier. He was met by
Bayard, who commanded a detachment of 1200 men-at-
arms, and not a single foot-soldier. The English prince,
alarmed at this, dismounted, and made his lansquenets
surround him. Bayard absolutely wished to attack
them with his 1200 men-at-arms, and said to the Lord
of Fiennes, " Let us charge them. If we break them,
we shall have their king; if they drive us back, our
horses will carry us off without much loss."

Fiennes answered him, " Do so if you wish, but not
with my consent. I have orders from the king to guard
my country alone, and to risk nothing." So no attack
was made, and Bayard and his men had the vexation of
seeing the king of England and his escort pass. But at
last our hero could contain himself no longer. He fell
upon the rear of the troop, and soon put them to the
double-quick, so that in their hurry they left a large
piece of cannon, which they called St. John, being one of
twelve similar pieces, each bearing the name of an apostle,
and for that reason called by Henry his Twelve Apostles.

This king, a few days after his arrival at his camp, was there joined by the emperor, who brought him some troops from Hainault and Burgundy, and this arrival was celebrated by cannonades against the town. The King of France had come as far as Amiens, and sent word every day to his general to victual Terouana at any price, which was very difficult to do, because of the number of troops who invested it. However, to obey the king, they determined to do it. It was resolved that all the cavalry should go and give an alarm to the enemy's camp, and that by this diversion they would make it easier for those who were ordered to go to the other end of the town to throw pieces of bacon into the ditch, for the besieged to pick up. They tried to carry this plan into execution, but the enemies, informed by their spies, placed 12,000 English foot-soldiers, 4000 or 5000 lansquenets, and ten pieces of cannon in a favourable part, so that as soon as the French cavalry had passed to give the alarm, this body of troops sallied out and cut off their road; and at the place where he foresaw that the attack would be made, he had put all his cavalry in arms, with the Burgundians and Hainaulters.

On the French side they had received orders not to fight, but only to occupy the enemy, to second the transport of provisions into the town, and if the enemy showed themselves strong, to retire with all speed.

The order was pretty well executed, but did not succeed; for the French, having commenced the skirmish with spirit, and soon perceiving a body of troops coming to enclose them, sounded retreat, and every one galloped off to the camp. The first fell upon the companies that Chabannes and the Duke of Longueville commanded, and threw them all in disorder. The pursuers seeing this first small defeat, stuck to their point, and made the whole army turn their backs. Chabannes was energetic in trying to rally them, but in vain. "Turn, men-at-arms!" he cried. "It is only a false alarm." They did not listen to him; on the contrary, they fled at full speed towards the camp where were the foot-soldiers and the artillery. This adventure gave to the day's exploits the name of the Battle of Spurs.[2] The Duke of Longueville and Chabannes were made prisoners with some captains; but Chabannes escaped from the hands of those who took him.

Bayard, obliged to retire like the others, and to his great regret, often faced about upon the enemy with about fifteen men-at-arms of his company, and repulsed them. He found a little bridge over a very deep current of water which crossed the plain. Now this bridge was so narrow that only two men abreast could cross it. "My friends," he cried, "let us stop here, and take care of this bridge. I promise you that the enemy shall not wrest it from us in an hour." He then sent a man of his troop to Chabannes, to tell him where he was, and to say that he would stop the enemy until Chabannes should send him help, and that, seeing the disorder in which the English were, it would be easy to defeat them. The Burgundians and Hainaulters were soon there, and, surprised at seeing themselves stopped by so few men, they charged them with all their forces. Bayard showed his customary bravery, and would have given the French time to rally and come to him, when

---

[2] M. de Voltaire, in his general History, calls the Battle of Spurs a *complete* defeat. All the contemporary historians say that the retreat of the French was an ordered retreat; that there was none or very little blood shed, and, looking at it in the light of a flight, we must agree that it was not only voluntary, but very wise.

he perceived a troop of 200 horses, which gained the lower part of the current and crossed it near a mill. Seeing himself shut in in front and in the rear without any means of escape, he said to his comrades :—

"Let us give ourselves up. These forces are too strong, and we are too few. They are at least in the proportion of ten to one, and all our prowess will be of no use to us, for our horses are overcome with fatigue, and our men too far off to help us, and if these English archers reach us they will cut us to pieces."

His advice was followed, and every one gave himself up to the nearest of the enemy's troops. Bayard, whose presence of mind never left him, perceived a well-equipped officer who had retired under the trees to rest and refresh himself; he was unarmed, and his sword was beside him. Our knight ran to him, and snatching up his sword and putting it to his throat, said to him :—

"Give yourself up, man-at-arms, or you die!"

The knight, much astonished at being taken by surprise in this manner, did not wish to die there. He gave himself up saying :—

"As I am without defence, I render my sword and my person to you; but tell me to whom I have given myself up."

"To Captain Bayard," replied the knight, "who is himself your prisoner, and there is my sword."

The gentleman understood nothing of the adventure yet, but Bayard informed him of it all, and made his condition that if it happened that the English wished to kill him, he should give up his arms to him. The officer agreed to this, and kept his word, for they had to defend themselves against some scouts who amused themselves by killing the prisoners, when they found nothing more to plunder.

At last they arrived at the camp of the King of England, where the officer lodged his prisoner in his tent, and treated him as a man who honoured valour even in his enemy. That lasted four or five days, at the end of which Bayard said to him one morning with a very serious air:—

"My worthy gentleman, I am beginning to tire of being here doing nothing; you will oblige me much if you will have me taken to the camp of the king, my master."

"What," said the Burgundian, "eh? You have said nothing about your ransom yet."

"Nor you of yours," replied Bayard. "Are you not my prisoner? Did I not have it in my power to slay you? and if I gave myself up to you, was it for any other reason than to save my life? I have your word, and you will keep it; if not, sooner or later, I shall fight you."

The gentleman, more astonished than before, did not know what answer to make to him; he knew his name too well to wish to fight him. However, he said:—

"Sir captain, I will abide by the judgment of those to whom we report our case."

The emperor, having heard that Bayard was in the camp, and seeing the joy that his capture caused everybody, almost as great as the gain of a battle, sent for him, and received him with extraordinary kindness.

"Captain Bayard, my friend," said he, "the sight of you gives me great joy. Would to God that I had many such men as you! It seems to me that if such were the case, I should not be long in requiting the king your master for the good turns he has done me in times past. But," added he, "it appears to me that when we were in battle together I had heard it said that Bayard never fled."

"Sire," replied the knight, "if I had fled, I should now not be here."

Then he reminded the emperor on what occasions he had been in battle with him. Just then the King of England arrived, and he also received Bayard in a most gracious manner. Afterwards he joked with him upon the precipitate retreat of the French, and said that he had never seen such a good run. The emperor was also rather witty in his remarks; but Bayard interrupted them by saying that the French men-at-arms were not to blame, because they had had express orders not to fight.

"They had," added he, "neither foot-soldiers nor artillery, and it was doubtful whether your majesties would not bring all your forces, which indeed happened; and they know that the French nobility enjoy a settled reputation; not that I place myself among their number, though."

"You!" replied the King of England. "I think that if all the French gentlemen were your equals, the siege that I have put before Terouana would soon be raised. But you are our prisoner."

"Saving the respect I owe to your majesties," said Bayard, "I cannot allow that I am a prisoner, and I beg you to be judges in the case."

And then, in presence of the gentleman, he related the transaction as it had occurred, and the officer could not deny any of the statement. The two princes appeared to consult each other by their looks, and the emperor declared that Bayard was not a prisoner, and that the Burgundian was rather his; but that, considering all things, they should be quits, and the knight should have the liberty of returning to his camp when the King of England should allow him. That prince was ready to ratify the emperor's judgment, and said that if Bayard remained six weeks on parole without bearing arms he would allow him to visit all the towns of Flanders, and afterwards give him leave to depart. The knight, with one knee on the ground, thanked the two princes for their decision, and a few days after left them to avail himself of their permission to visit the country.

The King of England secretly proposed to him to enter into his service, assuring him that he would load him with riches and honours. Pope Julius had proposed the same thing to him at the end of 1503, after the exploit at the Garilliano, promising also to make him Captain-general of the Church; but he had only one answer to give to both, namely, " that he had only one master in heaven, who was God, and one upon earth, who was the King of France, and that he would never serve any other."

We have already said that although Bayard was not rich, yet there was no man who kept a better table than he wherever he went. As soon as he arrived in Flanders, he gave fêtes to the ladies, and regaled the emperor's subjects so well and so often, and especially gave them such good wine, although it was dear, that he sent them away quite satisfied, and they wanted nothing but their beds when they left his house. They would very much have liked this style of life to last longer, but as soon as the term had expired Bayard took leave of them, and was taken in safety to within a short distance of the French camp.

The town of Terouana was continuously cannonaded, and neither being supplied with men or provisions it was finally reduced to capitulation. The articles were that all the soldiers should leave with bag and baggage, that no wrong should be done to the inhabitants, and that the town should not be destroyed. The first article was strictly observed, but the others were not; for the King of England, after having battered down the walls, set fire to the town in various places. The ruin of this town was completed in the reign of Henry II., and in 1553 by Charles V., and now scarcely a vestige of it remains.

The taking of the town of Tournay followed that of Terouana. It fell into the hands of the English by the fault of the garrison, which refused to receive a reinforcement of French troops, thinking itself strong enough without assistance for the defence. The winter separated the armies; the King of England and the emperor returned to their states, and the French were scattered in various garrisons in Picardy and the neighbouring provinces.

In the course of this same year, 1513, the Swiss, led by the Lord of Verzi, and accompanied by a body of lansquenets, to the number of 30,000 men, made a descent upon Burgundy, where was the governor of the province, the brave Louis de la Trimouille, who, having no troops to oppose them, was obliged to shut himself up in Dijon, where he hoped to stop this large army, but the town was soon cannonaded with fury and besieged on both sides. The governor did his duty nobly, being day and night upon the ramparts; but at last the breaches were made, and seeing himself surrounded by a very few men, and without hope of help, he saw not only that his town was lost if he persisted in defending it, but the danger which all the kingdom would be in at the loss of the place, as there was no other place of defence between Dijon and Paris. Seeing that there was no other course to pursue, he had the wisdom to treat secretly with the Swiss.

He reminded them of the advantages that they had

already received from the Kings of France, and the great benefit that they would always find in an alliance with this crown ; he made them fair promises, and took upon himself the task of negotiating the alliance between themselves and the king; he made them plainly see that they had everything to lose and nothing to gain by desolating the kingdom; in short, he treated so well and so ably, after having agreed to give them a large sum of money,[3] that they returned, taking with them La Trimouille's hostages, the Lord of Mairières, his nephew, the young Rochfort, son of Guy of Rochfort, Chancellor of France, and some notables of the town.

This treaty of the Lord of La Trimouille was not approved by everybody at the court, where jealousy often distorts the finest actions; but the blame was not slow to be changed into praise, and then, and since, all the historians have reported this action as one of the greatest services which could have been rendered to any of our kings.

Louis XII. during his stay at Amiens had the annoyance of learning of the defeat and death of his relative and ally James IV., King of Scotland, who, trying to enter England with a large army, was conquered in battle[4] by the Duke of Norfolk, and left dead on the field.

Winter quarters having been taken, the king went to Blois, to which place he was attached, as it was his birthplace. Here he hoped to be able to rest from the fatigues

---

[3] Puffendorff says 10,000 crowns, which would be worth more than a million of our present money.

[4] It is scarcely necessary to say that this battle was the well-known Flodden, that Scott has popularized by "Marmion."

and annoyances that he had undergone during the whole year; but it was not to be.

The court was hardly established at Blois, when the Queen of France, Anne, Duchess of Brittany, was seized with a disease which was at once declared to be mortal, so that all the skill of the doctors could not prevent her death, which happened eight days after, at the commencement of January,[5] 1513, at the age of thirty-eight years.

She left two daughters, Madame Claude, who, a short time after, married Francis, Count of Angoulême, who, in the end, succeeded to the crown, and Madame Renée, wife of Hercules II, Duke of Ferrara.[6]

In the month of October following (1514) the king married again. His bride was Mary, sister to the King of England. It was the Duke of Longueville, made prisoner at Terouana, and taken to England, who negotiated this alliance, for the consummation of which the king did not appear in a hurry. But he wished for peace. His finances were exhausted, his troops diminished, and he feared, above all things, to oppress his people by taxation.

The princess was taken to Abbeville, and thence to Paris, where she was received with astonishing magni-

---

[5] The month of January was then the tenth month in the year. The year began at Easter, whatever date it fell upon; the year began to be dated from the 1st of January, in 1564, by order of Charles IX.

[6] She embraced the doctrines of Calvin, who went to Ferrara for the express purpose of bringing about her conversion. This change in her religion not allowing her to remain in Italy, she returned to France in the following reign. Francis I. gave her the Duchy of Montargis for appanage. She died there in 1568, without being reconciled to the Church of Rome.

ficence.[7] The king had the kindness to change his mode of life in favour of his young wife; he enjoyed pleasures, and attended fêtes with her, and often carried them far into the night, so that instead of getting up, and going to bed early, as he had been accustomed to do, he gave himself up to a mode of life which shortened his days. He died after a year of widowhood, and three months of his second marriage, on the 1st of January, 1514. He was a good prince, and much lamented by his people, who embalmed his memory for ever by bestowing on him the surname of *Father of the People*. By the death of Louis the crown passed by right to the Count of Angoulême,[8] who was twenty years old, and a son-in-law of Louis. He was conducted to Rheims, and consecrated with a pomp of which there is no previous example. The fêtes began again on his entrance into Paris, where he remained till Easter, and during this interval he made his treaty of peace, through the mediation of Charles, Archduke of Austria, Count of Flanders, who was to marry Madame Renée, sister to the queen. This marriage was broken off at the peace a short time after, and she married the Duke of Ferrara, as we have said. The Queen of France, widow of Louis XII, married the Duke of Suffolk, and returned

---

[7] It was then the custom to give a triumphal reception to kings and queens, which were very sumptuous and very magnificent for those times. The custom ceased in Henry the Second's reign. The route of these grand entries was always through the gate and street of St. Denis.

[8] He was a grandson of John, Duke of Orleans, who was the son of Louis I, also Duke of Orleans, and Valentina of Milan. Louis I. was brother to the King Charles VI. He was assassinated by order of the Duke of Burgundy. Francis I, as the great-grandson of Valentina of Milan, had, through her, the same claims upon this duchy as Louis XII.

to England. The Duke of Bourbon was made Constable of France at twenty-six years of age; and his sister married the Duke of Lorraine, Anthony I.

(1515.) The new king did not give himself completely up to pleasure; he meditated re-conquering his Duchy of Milan, which the Sforzas continued to hold in sovereignty. He ordered the troops to come secretly by the Lyonnais into Dauphiny, where Bayard (whom he had made lieutenant-general of the province) was awaiting them. He sent orders for them to advance into the lands of the Marquisate of Saluces, where the Lord Prospero Colonna was with the troops, and the title of lieutenant-general of the pope, and treated these lands as conquered country, excepting one place called Ravel, strong enough to hold out against him.

We have seen, in the course of this history, that Bayard was always the first on an expedition, and the last at a retreat. We will give an account of his first endeavours in the country. He knew at first that this Prospero Colonna had with him 300 men-at-arms, and a number of light horse, all perfectly mounted; he also knew where he ordinarily lodged, and resolved to surprise him. He had with him his company of 100 men-at-arms, and from 300 to 400 foot-soldiers, but he had not enough cavalry to carry out his plan, in which the infantry were of no service. He wrote to the Constable de Bourbon at Briançon, telling him this, and the constable sent word to the king, who was already at Grenoble, and who ordered three of his bravest captains (Chabannes, Humbercourt and D'Aubigny), to join him with their companies.

As soon as Bayard knew they were on the road, he entered Piedmont with his men-at-arms only, but Colonna, knowing their small number, did not disturb himself, and remained quiet. The knight communicated his plan to two Piedmontese gentlemen, to surprise the town of Carmagnola. Indeed, as soon as the reinforcement arrived, Bayard assembled the captains, and showed them that there was no time to lose, because, if Colonna were informed of their number, he would not wait for them, or perhaps he would call the Swiss to his aid, " who are," said he, " in large numbers at Pignerol and Saluces. For that reason," he continued, " my advice is that you give your horses time for repose and refreshment to-night, and to-morrow we will march at break of day. It is true we shall have a stream of water to pass, but the Lord of Morète, who is here now, and who knows the country, will show you a ford where you can cross without danger." Every one went to take a few hours' rest, and between two and three o'clock in the morning all were on horseback, and marched away as quietly as possibly.

Colonna was in Carmagnola; but having the fixed notion that Bayard had only his own company, he would not have sallied out so soon, but that the same night that the French were making their plans to surprise him at break of day, he received orders to go to Pignerol to assist at a council which was to be held there, to talk of the news they had received of the march of the troops from France. He set out then pretty early, and well accompanied, to go and dine at a little town named Villafranca on the Po, at seven or eight miles from Carmagnola. When Bayard's company arrived at the castle of the last-named town, they learnt that Prospero had only left it a quarter of an hour, and they were informed of the road he had taken. It would be difficult to express the vexation of everybody at losing such a chance. The captains deliberated as to the part they had to perform, some wished to go forward, others were undecided; but Bayard reassured them, saying: "As we have come so far, I propose that we follow them, and if we overtake them in open field, it must be some great misfortune indeed which will prevent our leaving some there."

All agreed with him, and said it was necessary to set out immediately; but before doing so the Lord of Morète alone, and disguised, was sent on before, to discover the enemy's situations. Morète acquitted himself well and quickly, and told them, on his return, that Colonna and his whole escort were going to dine at Villafranca in the greatest security. They immediately agreed upon the order of their march. Humbercourt was to go first with 100 archers; Bayard, at a bow-shot's distance, should follow him with 100 men-at-arms; Chabannes and D'Aubigny bringing up the rear with the remainder of the troop.

In the mean time Prospero Colonna had received information from one of his spies that the French were in the fields in large numbers. "I know what it is," he replied, "it is only Captain Bayard and his company, at least if the others have not flown over the mountains."

A moment afterwards another spy came and said to him: "My lord, the French are quite close to us with more than 1000 horse."

This second piece of news staggered him a little, and calling one of his gentlemen, he said to him: "Take twenty knights with you, follow the road to Carmagnola, and see what is going on, and come and tell me." Then he sent his quarter-master to go and prepare his men at Pignerol, and sat down to table.

In the meantime the French troop was nearing them,

according to the plan that had been agreed upon; the first, being at about a mile and a-half from Villafranca, discovered the gentleman whom Prospero had sent to bring news of them. As soon as he and his escort caught sight of the French, they turned their backs and retraced their steps at full speed. Humbercourt and his men pursued them at full speed, after informing Bayard of what had happened, who immediately followed in their train. Humbercourt reached the fugitives as they were entering the town, and about to close the gate; but he and his men crying "France! France!" hindered their doing so, and did marvellous feats of arms, without any accident, excepting a slight wound that Humbercourt received in the face. Bayard, who had soon joined him, with much clatter and noise, made himself master of the gate.

The quarter-master, who heard this noise as he left the town by the opposite gate, returned, and put himself in defence, but he was soon conquered, and part of his men slain. Chabannes and D'Aubigny, who were close behind Bayard, put a guard at the first gate, and went themselves to take care of the second (for there were only two), so that no one should leave it; but notwithstanding these precautions, two Albanians crossed the small plank of the drawbridge, and ran to a troop of 4000 Swiss, telling them of the danger Prospero was in. While he was gone, Prospero was surrounded, and attacked in the house where he was dining. He tried at first to defend himself; but when he saw the large number of assailants, and heard the names of the captains who were against him, he saw that resistance was useless, and gave himself up with great regret, in despair at having been surprised there, instead of waiting for the French in the open field.

Bayard, who was as generous in victory as he was brave in action, said to him to console him: "Lord Prospero, it is the fate of war; we gain one day and lose the next; but you tell me that you wish you had met me in the open field; thank God that he did not permit it, for I assure you that, seeing the courage of our men, you and yours would have been troubled to escape us."

"I would to God," replied Prospero, coldly, "that it had happened so. I would willingly have fallen on the field."

With him were taken three captains, the Count of Policastro, Pierre Morgant, and Charles Cadamastro. Afterwards the French began to plunder their baggage and effects.

The booty was considerable considering the few men who were taken; and, if they had been careful, they would have had above the worth of 100,000 ducats; but there were many things broken and lost. The most valuable part of the booty was the horses, of which there were nearly 700, and, amongst the number, 400 Spanish horses of remarkable beauty. Prospero confessed to them that, for his part, he lost more than 50,000 ducats' worth in gold and silver vessels, jewels, and coined money. The French could not carry all away, for they were informed that the Swiss were coming to attack them, and that they were not far off. Hearing that, they had retreat sounded, everyone seizing what he could carry off most easily. They made the prisoners march before the troop, and retired.

As they left the town by one gate, the Swiss entered by the other. They had both horse and foot soldiers; but they did not pursue the French. Thus finished this expedition, of which Bayard had the honour both of the planning and success, and in which Prospero Colonna was taken prisoner by a man whom he had boasted he would take sooner or later, like a bird in a cage. The king in the meantime, at the head of his army, had already advanced far over the mountains, which no army had ever crossed before. At the mountain of Santa Paolo he received the news of the taking of Prospero. This intelligence gave him great pleasure, for he knew Prospero to be a valiant man, and if he had been present at the battle which was given a short time after, he would have had with him at least 1000 men-at-arms, some Spanish, and some belonging to the pope, who would have been powerful enough to decide the victory.

CHAPTER XXIII.

THE king having crossed the mountains, descended into Piedmont, and passed through Turin, where he was received by the Duke of Savoy in a manner befitting his dignity as King of France, and as a near relation and ally of the Duke. The Swiss, who were posted in various parts to bar their progress, having heard of the overthrow of Prospero Colonna, took the road to Milan, with the French at their heels. While these events were occurring, a truce was proposed, and looked upon even as already concluded. That gave an opportunity to the Duke of Gueldres, an ally of France, who had brought 10,000 lansquenets to the king's assistance, to return to his country, leaving his troops under the orders of the Duke of Guise (Claude of Lorraine, brother of the reigning duke), and of his lieutenant, the Captain Michel. The king approached to within twelve or fifteen miles of Milan, where the Swiss were established. But the negotiations were broken by the wickedness of the Cardinal of Sion.[1] He was a sworn enemy of France,

---

[1] Matthew Schiner, or, according to others, Schaner, Bishop of Sion, in the Valais, a mortal enemy of the French name. He died a short time after this exhibition of anger.

and now, gave a fatal proof of his hatred. He was at Milan, and feared that, by the treaty then negotiating, this duchy would fall into the king's hands. Whilst Lautrec had gone to Galénas, to carry the necessary preliminary money, he convened the Swiss, and harangued them with so much rage and fury, that they took up arms, left the town, and went like madmen to attack the king's camp, which was not prepared for this violent incursion. The constable who was in the vanguard quickly put himself on the defensive, and the king, who had just sat down to table, left it to go to the help of his men. The skirmish had already begun, and many were dead on both sides. The king's lansquenets, wishing to signalize themselves by a bold stroke, and throw themselves on the Swiss, tried to cross a ditch, which was before the French camp; but when they had crossed it to the number of between 700 and 800, the Swiss attacked them on the flank, and drove the greater part of them into the ditch. The slaughter would have been immense, if the Duke of Guise, the constable, the Count of St. Pol, Bayard, and several others, had not gone to their assistance, and driven back the Swiss. The Duke of Guise was left for dead in this action. The vanguard routed the enemy, 2000 of whom, in their flight, passed before the king, who charged them briskly, and killed many; but he was in danger of losing his life, for he had his buff coat pierced with a halberd stroke.

The night separated the combatants, who did not meet again. Every one retired to his own side, and remained under arms till day, the king remaining on horseback with the meanest of the soldiers.

In the last charge upon the Swiss a strange adventure happened to Bayard, in which he marvellously escaped losing his life. He was mounted on a spirited horse, who, feeling himself wounded with many pikes, slipped his bridle, and not feeling the bit, took his course right through the Swiss, and would have carried his rider into another troop which would have given him no quarter. By good fortune, the horse became entangled in some vine-stocks hanging from one tree to another, according to the Italian custom, and there he was obliged to stop. If Bayard was ever in fear for his life it was then; however, he preserved his customary presence of mind. He slid from his horse to the ground, left all his armour, and creeping on his hands and feet so as to escape observation, turned to the direction whence he heard cries of "France! France!" and arrived in safety at the king's camp, thanking God with all his heart for his deliverance from so great a danger.

The first man he met was the Duke of Lorraine, by whom he was particularly beloved and esteemed. The duke was much astonished to see him on foot, unarmed, and in such a plight. Bayard related his adventure to him, and the prince immediately gave him a splendid horse, which he had received as a present from Bayard, who gained it at the first taking of Brescia.[2]

---

[2] "This horse," says the Loyal Servant, "was named *Le Carinau*, and had been formerly presented to the duke by Bayard himself, who had won him at the taking of Brescia. He (the horse) was left for dead after the battle of Ravenna, when the good knight leapt from off his back, by reason that he had two pike wounds in the flanks, and more than twenty gashes in the head from swords; but next day he was found grazing, and began to neigh; in consequence of which he was brought back to the good knight's quarters, and there healed. Incredible things are told respecting him: he suffered himself to be handled like any human being, probes to be put into his wounds with-

Bayard, mounted once more, was grieved at being without his helmet, not only because he was so heated with walking that he was in danger of taking a violent cold without it, but he did not consider the battle over yet. At this moment he saw near him a gentleman, a friend of his, who had his helmet carried by his page; he borrowed it of him, resolved not to return it till after the battle, which had begun at daybreak, and did not end until nearly mid-day.

The Swiss at first directed their attacks against the French artillery, who destroyed a great number of them. The fight was fierce and bloody on both sides; at last they were entirely defeated, and left 10,000 or 12,000 of their men on the field. The rest withdrew towards Milan, fighting their way, and in pretty good order. They were pursued both by the French and Venetians, whom the seignory had sent to the king, commanded by the noble Bartholomew d'Alviani, who lost several of his best officers, amongst others the young Petigliano.[3] The French also lost many illustrious men, such as the Count of St. Pol, the brave Humbercourt, the Count of Saucerre, and Lord of Muy, the Prince of Salmon (cadet of Louis de la Trimouille), and the Count of Bussy, brother of the late grand master of Chaumont, who was wounded there, and died soon after.

The Swiss did not remain long at Milan. The day

---

out stirring, and ever after, when a sword chanced to meet his eyes, he would run and seize it fiercely with his teeth. Was never seen a more courageous horse, not even excepting Alexander's courser, Bucephalus."—*From the translation by Robert Southey.*

[3] He belonged, as also the Count Petigliano, whom we have so often mentioned, to the illustrious house of the Ursino at Rome.

after their defeat they commenced their journey to their own country. The king was undecided whether he should send troops after them to put an end to them; but he concluded that it was better to let them go, foreseeing that he might require them in the end; but if he had wished, not a single one would have returned whence he came. So much for the success which attended the charitable harangue of the Cardinal of Sion.

On the evening of the same day, during supper, the king talked a great deal of this battle and of those who had distinguished themselves in it. All voices united to give the palm to the knight Bayard, who, as he always did, had performed noble and valiant deeds, and who received from the king the most glorious reward that a subject can hope for from his prince. The king wished to receive the order of knighthood from his hands. Bayard excused himself with his ordinary modesty, saying that such honour did not belong to him, but rather to princes of the blood, or other great lords, who had distinguished themselves more than he had. But the king was determined, and ordered him to do his bidding, in these words :—

"Before bestowing the honour of knighthood on those who have distinguished themselves in battle, I must myself receive that honour from one who is a knight; for which reason, Bayard, my friend, I wish to be knighted by your hand this day, because he who has fought on foot and on horseback better than all others is reputed the most worthy knight. It is thus with you, who have fought in many battles against many nations. So, Bayard, make haste, and quote neither laws nor canons. Do my will and command, if you wish to be amongst the number of my good servants and subjects."

"I can only obey," replied Bayard, and taking his

sword, he said: "Sire, may this be as efficacious as if done by Roland, or Oliver, Godfrey, or Baldwin, his brother." Then he performed the ceremony, and added: "In good truth, you are the first prince that ever was made a knight. God grant that in battle you may never fly." Then, having kissed his sword, and holding it in his right hand, he said: "Glorious sword, that to-day hast had the honour of knighting the greatest king in the world, I will only employ thee in future against the infidels, enemies of the Christian name. In truth, my good sword, thou shalt be kept as a sacred relic, and honoured above all others." Then he made two leaps, and replaced his sword in its scabbard.[4]

This sword has unfortunately been lost.[5] Charles Emanuel, Duke of Savoy, wished to have it as a relic of great value, and asked the heirs of Bayard for it after his death. Not succeeding in getting that, he obtained his mace from Charles of Motet, Lord of Chichiliano, one of his heirs, to whom he wrote thanking him, saying, "that, mingled with the satisfaction that he felt at placing this treasure in the best place in his gallery, was a feeling of grief that it should not still remain in such good hands as those of its original owners."

Maximilian Sforza, who claimed to be the legitimate Duke of Milan as his father's heir, retired into the castle after the defeat of the Swiss; but as soon as he saw the preparations for besieging it, he gave it up, and left it with his men.

The king, enjoying a little more tranquillity, went to

---

[4] According to the Memoirs of Fleuranges, Bayard conferred the honour of knighthood on Francis I. *before* the battle; other historians agree with the Loyal Servant, and say *after*.

[5] See additional note at the end of this volume.

Bologna to see Pope Leo X, who gave him a magnificent reception; and after a short stay he returned to Milan, whence shortly afterwards he travelled to his kingdom, leaving the constable, the Duke of Bourbon, as his lieutenant-general.

Francis I. entered his kingdom through Provence, where he was met by the queen, his wife, and Madame de Beaujeu, his mother, whom he had appointed regent before he set out for Italy.

Just at this time (the 23rd of January, 1515) died Ferdinand, King of Arragon, the husband of the late incomparable Isabella, Queen of Castille. They only left one daughter, known as Jeanne la Folle, then the widow of Philip le Beau, Archduke of Austria, and the mother of Charles V. and Ferdinand I, both emperors.

A short time afterwards died John d'Albret, King of Navarre, whose kingdom Ferdinand had usurped, as we have seen in the course of this narrative.[6]

---

[6] In his will he ordered that his body should be placed in the tomb of the royal house at Pampeluna, although this town belonged to the King of Spain; not that he imagined he should be obeyed, but he did it in order to maintain a tone of sovereignty over the town and his usurped kingdom of Navarre.

CHAPTER XXIV.

HE emperor, 1516, jealous of the victory that the king had gained, and which made him master of Milan, assembled a very large number of lansquenets, with Swiss from the canton of Zurich, and the Grisons, and marched in person towards the Duchy of Milan. The constable, not having sufficient troops to go and meet him, shut himself up in his town with his army; but having a few days afterwards received a reinforcement of 8000 or 10,000 Swiss, the emperor did not give him time to give him battle, but went away quicker than he came, leaving a goodly number of his soldiers as prisoners of war. He died in the following year, and was succeeded by his grandson, Charles V, already King of Spain in right of his mother Jeanne la Folle.

The King of France had the satisfaction of seeing himself father of a dauphin, born in the town of Amboise on the last day of February. The news of the birth of this child was received with universal joy. He died a dauphin in the year 1536.

(1519-1522). Francis I, having no cause of quarrel with the new emperor, was remaining quiet, and enjoying the pleasures of the court, when an unforeseen event happened to disturb peace.

The Lord of Sedan, Robert de la Marck, of whom we have spoken before, and who was in the service of France, made inroads upon Charles' territory, without any apparent cause for such an unjust attempt. The emperor soon got ready more troops than were necessary to reduce so feeble an enemy, and to make himself master of the country. His army consisted of 40,000 men, commanded by two brave generals, Henry, Count of Nassau, and the Lord of Sickengen, with 110 pieces of cannon. This army overran the territories of the Lord of Sedan, took from him four places, Floranges, Bouillon, Messancourt, and Soignes. Some others defended themselves; but Sedan and Jametz were not besieged, being almost impregnable. This expedition gave umbrage to the King Francis I.

He could not calmly stand by and see his province of Champagne at the mercy of so formidable an army, so he sent his brother-in-law, the Duke d'Alençon, with a number of cavalry, to that frontier, and went himself to Rheims.

The Imperialists affected not to give any sign of hostility, paying strictly for all they bought from the French territories, and their general, the Count of Nassau, keeping strict order there, being expressly bidden to do so by the emperor, who wished, he said, to maintain peace with the king.

However, all at once, and without any declaration of war, the Imperialists laid siege to Monzon, of which place the Lord of Montmort, grand equerry of Brittany, was governor, who, having only his company and some few foot-soldiers, was not in a state to defend a place surprised, and bare of provisions and artillery.

What was still more unfortunate for him was, that although he had the courage to defend it to the last breath, his men refused service, and forced him to give it up on condition that their lives should be saved. Some of them wished to make him appear criminal to the king, as not having done his duty; but those who understood the ways of war gave him justice, especially those who knew that he would rather have buried himself under the ruins than such a misfortune should have happened.

This event made the king uneasy for Champagne, and as the town of Mézières was the nearest to Monzon, he considered that it was also the first to be taken care of, so much the more, because, if it had been taken, Champagne was defenceless. He immediately sent to the knight Bayard, as the man in whom he placed most confidence, and the one most capable of defending the place long enough to put him in a condition to assemble an army, and make head against that of the emperor.

When Bayard arrived a council of war was held, at which he assisted. The state of the town of Mézières was taken into consideration, the proximity of the enemy's army, and the impossibility of providing troops and furnishing them with provisions and artillery immediately. The result of their conference was that they should burn Mézières and devastate the environs to starve the hostile army. But Bayard was opposed to such a proceeding, and said to the king: "Sire, no place is weak where there are men capable of defending it." And he offered to go and do his best with the town.

The king gave him the commission, and sent orders to the Duke d'Alençon, the governor of the province, to supply him with all that he wanted, men, artillery, provisions, and ammunition.

Bayard had never undertaken a charge which gave him more pleasure, nor a better opportunity of serving his master and acquiring honour. He betook himself in all diligence to Mézières, with the Duke of Lorraine's company of 100 men-at-arms, whom he commanded as his lieutenant, and with his chosen captains, Charles Alleman, Lord of Laval, and Peter Terrail, Lord of Bernin, his cousins; Antoine de Clermont, Viscount Tallard; Francis de Sassenage Ennard, Guiffrey, Beaumont, and others, all from Dauphiny, and the flower of the nobility, who all brought their companies with them.

Anne of Montmorency, then twenty-eight years old, and afterwards grand master and constable of France, wished to follow him with his company of men-at-arms, "doing himself the honour," as he said, " of serving under so great and renowned a captain." Many other gentlemen imitated this good example, and joined Bayard to learn the art of war from him; amongst others were Captain Boccara, of the house of Reffuge, and the Lord of Montmoreau, who each brought him 1000 foot-soldiers.

On his arrival, he found the place not in a condition to sustain the siege, which was expected that day or the next. His first care was to send away across the bridge of the Meuse all the useless mouths,[1] and to destroy the

---

[1] Useless mouths, i. e. men who would eat but not fight. Bayard seems to have taken the same view of these lazy drones in war as Milton in the church:—

—— Such as for their bellies' sake,
Creep and intrude, and climb into the fold!
Of other care they little reckoning make,
Than how to scramble at the shearers' feast,
And shove away the worthy bidden guest!
Blind mouths!—LYCIDAS, l. 114.

bridge as soon as they were outside. After that he assembled all the principal townspeople and the chief men of the garrison he found there, and made them swear not to talk of giving up the place, but to defend it to the death. "And if we are in want of provisions," added he, laughing, "we will eat our horses and our boots." Then he ordered that the parts that were fortified should be repaired, and that fortifications should be made where there were none; and to give courage to the workers, he was the first to put his hand to the work, and distributed more than 6000 crowns of his own money amongst them.

"Comrades," he said, "shall it be said that the town was lost by our faults, seeing what a gallant company of brave men we make here altogether? It seems to me that if we were in a meadow, with only a ditch four feet wide before us, that we could fight a whole day without being defeated. Thank God, we have ditches, walls, and a rampart, and before our enemy plants his foot there I think many will be sleeping in the ditches."

In short, he so encouraged his men that all thought they were quite invincible, having him for a leader.

Two days after his arrival, the siege was laid on both sides the Meuse, on one side by Captain Sickengen with 14,000 or 15,000 men, and on the other side by the Count of Nassau with more than 20,000. The next day they sent a herald to summon Bayard to give the place up to them. The herald, being introduced into the town, delivered his message, which was to inform the commander, on the part of his masters, that it was impossible to resist them long, that they esteemed the great and praiseworthy chivalry that was in him, but that it would be marvellously annoying if they were taken by assault, for his honour would thereby be lessened, and possibly it might cost him his life. In fine, if he would give himself up, they would make as good a capitulation as he could wish. Bayard, to these propositions replied, smiling, "That he was not aware he had the honour of being known to the Lords of Nassau and of Sickengen, that he thanked them for their gracious offers; but that, as the king had chosen him to guard the place, he would take care of it so well that they should be tired of the siege before he was, and that so far from thinking of leaving it, he hoped to make a bridge of dead bodies in the ditches over which they could pass out." The herald took his leave with this answer, and repeated it to his masters in the presence of a French captain, named John Picard, who said to them, "My lords, I know this Captain Bayard. I have served under him. Do not expect to enter this place while he is living; he is a man who gives heart to the most cowardly. I assure you that he and his men would die at the breach before letting us put foot inside the town, and for my part, I wish there were 2000 more soldiers in the place rather than this Bayard."

"Captain Picard," answered the Count of Nassau, "is this Bayard of bronze or steel? If he is so brave, let him get ready to give us an opportunity of seeing him; for in the next four days I will send him so many cannon shots that he won't know which way to turn."

"All in good time," said Picard, "but you won't have it all your own way."

Immediately upon that the two generals ordered batteries of cannon, each one from his side, and were so well obeyed that in less than four days they had fired more than 5000 shots against the town. The besieged answered very well, but their artillery was small in comparison with that of their opponents. As soon as the Lord of Montmoreau's 1000 men heard the first play of these batteries they fled in spite of him, some by the gate, and the rest over the walls. When this flight was reported to Bayard, his answer was, " So much the better. I like such knaves better outside than in ; such rabble were not worthy to gain honour with us."

However, the town was greatly inconvenienced by the firing from Sickengen's quarters, for, as he had placed himself on a hill, he had a great advantage over it. Bayard, who not only was the bravest and wisest man of his age, but without his equal for expedients, thought of a very singular plan to dislodge Sickengen from his place, and this expedient succeeded. It was to write to the Lord Robert de la Marck, who was at Sedan, a letter, in which, after he had informed him that he was besieged on both sides, he added, " If I remember rightly, you told me a year ago that you proposed getting the Count of Nassau into the service of the king, our master, also that he is a relation of yours. I should wish such a thing to take place as much as you, because he has acquired the reputation of being very gallant. If you think such a change possible, I advise you to bring it about rather to-day than to-morrow, because before twenty-four hours have passed, he and his camp will be blown to pieces. I have news that 12,000 Swiss and 800 men-at-arms will sleep to-night at three leagues from here, who to-morrow at break of day will fall upon him, while on my side I shall make a vigorous onslaught, and fortunate will be he who escapes. I thought it my duty to warn you of this, trusting to you to keep my secret." When the letter was written, Bayard gave it in charge of a peasant, to whom he gave a crown, saying, " Go and carry this letter to the Lord of La Marck, who is at Sedan, three leagues from here, and give him the compliments of the writer, Captain Bayard."

The knight knew perfectly well that the peasant would be infallibly arrested on the way, as indeed he was, at two bow-shots from the town, and taken to Sickengen, who questioned him. The poor man thought his last moment had come. He was indeed in great danger of being hanged. "My lord," said he, "the great captain who is in our town has sent me to take this letter to the Lord of Sedan." And, taking it from a purse, he gave it up.

Sickengen opened it, and was strangely astonished at what it contained, and thought that the Count of Nassau, with whom he had had high words a short time before on the subject of the command, and whom he had refused to obey, wished, out of revenge, to do him a bad turn. "But," said he, swearing a fearful oath, "I will put a stop to his malice." Then he called for five or six of his captains, and gave them the letter to read. They were as indignant as he, thinking, like their general, that the count had put their camp on the other side of the Meuse on purpose to sacrifice them. Sickengen, without asking their advice, immediately had drums beaten to head quarters, sounded for assembly, and made them march off and cross the river.

The count, who heard the noise of this removal from his camp, sent a gentleman to know what it was. This messenger saw the body of the army in arms, and taking their way to the Meuse, he returned and told what he had seen. The count's surprise was great indeed, especially as he knew that to go away was to raise the siege. He sent a second time to beg Sickengen not to remove the camp till they had consulted together, that if he did so he would be acting contrary to his duty, and against the emperor's service. Sickengen coldly replied: "Go and tell the Count of Nassau that I am not his dupe, that I will not hold myself ready to be butchered for his sake, and that if he wishes to keep me from removing, we will see, he and I, to whom the field will remain." Nassau, who understood this answer still less than the first, and who thought that Sickengen was crossing the river to attack him, got his army ready for fight. Sickengen did the same as soon as he had crossed the river. Drums and trumpets made a deafening noise from both sides, and it seemed as if the two armies were about to rush upon each other.

However they calmed down, but the two generals, very much irritated, would neither see each other, nor speak, for eight days, and, in consequence, both left their camps, and went each his own way. Sickengen entered Picardy, and pushed his way to Guise, setting fire to everything on his way.

In time these generals were reconciled, but it was years before they discovered that they had both been equally duped.

It was a miracle that the bearer of the letter escaped from the danger which he had run, but he had the good fortune to return to Mézières, where he gave Bayard an account of all that had happened. He told him that he had been arrested, and his letter taken from him, that it had occasioned much noise and confusion, and that finally the enemies had soon decamped.

Bayard split his sides with laughing at the success of his stratagem, and in the excess of his joy he said: "As they would not open fire, I will." And at the same moment he sent five or six volleys of cannon into them at once. Thus the siege of Mézières was raised after having lasted three weeks, during which the besiegers had lost many men without having dared to give an assault. When the king heard of the raising of the siege of Mézières, and the artifice which Bayard had used, he felt much joy. He had only wished for time to assemble an army, which he could oppose to that of the emperor; and Bayard had doubled his hopes in procuring him this satisfaction, and delivering Champagne for him so well that the royal army was already on the frontier, and encamped at Fervagnes. The king went to join it, and our hero also went there to give him an account of what he had done, and on the way he retook Monzon.

CHAPTER XXV.

BAYARD was received by his prince with many marks of friendship and incredible praises. The king made him a knight of his order, and gave him, by an unexampled distinction, a company of 100 picked men-at-arms, an honour which only belonged to princes of the blood. All France resounded with the praises of Bayard, all agreeing that without his grand resistance at Mézières, the army of Charles V. would have penetrated into the heart of the kingdom still more easily, because in his seeming security, on the faith of the peace, Francis had not soldiers enough in a fit condition to stop 40,000 men; but he was revenged by following this army into Valenciennes, and if the Germans under Sickengen had done much damage in Picardy, the French rendered them double payment by their ravages in Hainault.

The departure of Bayard and his troops from the town of Mézières must have been a touching sight. The inhabitants accompanied them a long way with thanks and acclamations, they called them their defenders, their liberators, and kissed the arms and the coats of the soldiers. The happy event was celebrated in the town every year till the time of the revolution by a pompous fête, the chief part of the ceremony being the eulogium of Bayard.

As winter approached, the king went to Paris, and Bayard accompanied him. The public praises were renewed on his arrival; there was daily a concourse of great and small to see and congratulate him. Finally the French parliament put the finishing stroke to our hero's glory by sending him a deputation of presidents and councillors to compliment him upon the great service that he had just rendered to the king and the whole kingdom.

After making some stay at Paris, our knight, without fear, and without reproach, went to pass the winter at Grenoble, where it would be superfluous to tell of the reception that awaited him, and the fêtes that were made for him. Besides his quality as lieutenant-general of the province, he belonged to the highest nobility of Dauphiny, and this nobility felt it an honour to partake of the laurels with which he was crowned. They disputed as to who should have him in his turn, and came from the remotest parts of the province to see and admire him.

In the following spring, the king being at Compiègne, received news that the Genoese were about to rise, and that it would be as well to send a wise and prudent officer to them to keep them to their duty. Francis I. was not long in deciding. He sent at once to Bayard, whose wish to be useful, and attachment to his masters, he knew. When he had arrived, he gave him his commission and his orders, and finished in these words: "I beg you all in my power to undertake this expedition for love of me, having great faith in your presence."

Bayard, without delay, took the road to Grenoble, and immediately went thence to Genoa, where, during his stay, not only was everything quiet, but he made himself esteemed and respected by all, government, nobility, and common people.

He had brought with him his company of 100 men-at-arms, and 500 foot-soldiers, and he was accompanied by a number of gentlemen of the province, amongst others by Charles Alleman, by Balthazar de Beaumont, and the Lord of Romanèche. Having passed some time at Genoa, he went to join the Marshal of Foix, and the Lord Don Pedro of Navarre, of whom we have already spoken, and who had passed from the service of Spain to that of the king. They betook themselves together to the French army before Milan, under the orders of the famous Lautrec, also Marshal of France.

This campaign was not fortunate, for the Swiss having been driven back at the first attack in the battle of Bicoque, refused to return to the charge, and, a few days after, went back to their own country, which was the reason that the rest of the troops were put in garrison.

Bayard returned to the frontier of the Marquisate of Saluces, with his company and 2000 foot-soldiers, commanded by two lords of Dauphiny, Herculeys, and Vatilien, and there they waited till the enemy's troops were also garrisoned. Then he recrossed the mountains, and went to Grenoble, where he found that the plague had broken out. He had occasion to exercise his two favourite virtues, watchfulness and charity. He provided for all, nourished, at his expense, the poor sick people, or those suspected of being ill, and assisted them with doctors, surgeons, and medicine. He extended his cares and benefits to the monasteries and convents. In short, Bayard was, no doubt, the cause of the speedy cessation of this horrible scourge.

CHAPTER XXVI.

IN the following year (1523) the king, who had determined to regain his Duchy of Milan, resolved to go there and command an army in person; but the flight of Charles, Duke of Bourbon, Constable of France, who had embraced the emperor's cause, obliged him to change his plans, and he sent William Gouffier, Lord of Bonivet, Admiral of France, one of his favourites, to command in his place. Under him were many officers, and especially Bayard, whom he had no wish to forget.

Whilst the admiral laid siege to Milan, the knight marched towards Lodi with 8000 foot-soldiers, 400 men-at-arms, and eight pieces of cannon. His plan was to surprise the Duke of Mantua, Frederic de Gonzagua, who had taken possession of it. But this prince did not wait for him, the name of Bayard, and the knowledge that he was not far off, was enough for him. He left the town with great precipitation by the opposite gate.

Bayard entered Lodi without difficulty, put a garrison there, and immediately went to Cremona, which he besieged and cannonaded under the eyes of the Papal and Venetian troops, who dared not oppose it; and he would have made himself master of it if it had not been for the continual rain and storms which lasted four or five days without interruption, so that he was obliged to retire, not only because he was surrounded by the enemy, but because he feared provisions would fail, but little as he had, he supplied the garrison of the castle, which was on the king's side, both with men and provisions.

At the commencement of this year (1524), the king's army before Milan became weaker daily, while that of the emperor got stronger. The Admiral Bonivet came to establish his quarters in a little town named Biagras, and ordered Bayard to advance to a small village quite close to Milan, named Rebec, which had neither walls, nor ditches, nor barricades, and which was close to the camp of the enemy. He gave him 200 men-at-arms, and the 2000 men of the Lord of Lorges to keep those in the town on the alert, to cut off their provisions, and learn their news. Bayard, who, during the whole of his life, had only sought for occasions to serve the king, was too wide awake not to perceive the evident danger of the commission, he explained himself clearly enough to the general, showed him that the place was not tenable, and that the half of the army was not sufficient to guard it, and that, having nothing but shame to gain there, he begged him to reflect before sending him. But Bonivet, to quiet him, promised to send him some foot-soldiers to help him, assuring him that not a mouse could leave Milan that his spies did not inform him of it. Finally, whether by Bonivet's fair words, or his authority, he betook himself with his men to this miserable village of Rebec, where not only was there no fortification, but it was impossible to make any, excepting some barriers at the entrances.

When Bayard had arrived there, and saw for himself the danger of the post he occupied, he wrote letter after letter, asking for the reinforcement that the admiral had promised him, and which he never sent. Then he no longer doubted that this general had sent him there to perish, through jealousy or some other motive, for which he made up his mind to challenge him to mortal combat sooner or later.

The Spanish general, Don Ferdinand Francis d'Avalos, Marquis of Pescara, had a soldier named Lupon, of remarkable strength, and swiftness in running, who undertook to give him certain news of the state of the French at Rebec. This soldier, accompanied by a single arquebusier, went, unnoticed, to a French sentinel; he took the man round the waist, put him on his shoulders, and returned as swiftly as if he had had nothing to carry. They discharged some arquebuses at him, but his comrade prevented his being followed. Lupon took the Frenchman to the Marquis of Pescara, and stood him on his feet, so frightened that he was not able to speak. He was a man very much given to swearing; he gave himself to the devil a hundred times a day; and he thought now that the devil had taken him at his word, and come to fetch him away in good earnest.

At last, when he had recovered from his fright, with much time and trouble, he informed the marquis of Bayard's position, and of the number of his men. Upon this intelligence, the marquis determined to surprise the French the next night, and take our hero dead or alive.

He put in the fields, between twelve and one in the night, 7000 foot-soldiers and 1500 men-at-arms, guided by the men of the village, who knew all the avenues.

Bayard, who could not be easy at such a dangerous post, had watch kept in the night by half his men, he himself having passed three nights without sleeping. He fell ill with cold, and fatigue, and uneasiness of mind, and was so unwell that he was obliged to keep his room. He ordered some of his captains to keep watch and relieve each other, but they did nothing of the kind, and went to bed, only leaving three or four miserable archers on guard. The Spanish, who, for the sake of recognizing each other, all wore shirts outside their coats, approached the town, astonished at not meeting any one. Their first idea was that Bayard, informed of their plan, had retired to Biagras; but having gone about a hundred steps further on, they found the archers keeping watch, who immediately fled, crying, " Alarm! alarm!" The Spaniards followed them, and were at the barriers as soon as they. Bayard, who was fully sensible of the danger he was in, was sleeping fully dressed. He was soon astir and on horseback, and came to the barrier where the alarm was, accompanied by five or six of his men-at-arms. A moment after Captain de Lorges came to his assistance with his troop of foot-soldiers, who did wonders.

During the attack the Spaniards were running all over the village to find Bayard's lodging, for they only wanted to obtain possession of his person, and if they had been able to take him they would have returned as satisfied as if they had gained a complete victory. All the while they were looking for him he was defending the barrier, and from there he heard the noise of the drum, and judged of the number of the enemy's foot-soldiers. He resolved to retire as best he could, and said to the Captain de Lorges :—

" My companion and friend, our numbers are so unequal that if they pass the barriers we are all lost. Let us leave them our equipments, and save the men. Draw your men off, and march as close as you can, and I with my men-at-arms will form the rear-guard."

All that was well and successfully executed, with a loss of only nine or ten men, and about 150 horses, which were left to the enemy, with some grooms.

When the barrier was forced, the Spaniards searched all the houses, expecting to find the man they were in search of there; but Bayard was already at Biagras, where he had high words with the admiral, and if he had lived, he would certainly have taken sword in hand against him.

A little after this check, the admiral, who had not sufficient forces to resist those of the emperor, and who, on the contrary, saw his army decreasing every day by illness, assembled a council of war, of which the result was that there was nothing to do in the position in which they found themselves but to retire. They settled the order of the retreat, following which, the admiral and Bayard kept in the rear-guard, and so intimidated their enemies that they dared not approach, but saluted them from a distance, by discharging muskets, arquebuses, and small guns at them.

The next day the French continued to retreat, and their enemies to follow them. These last had placed upon the two borders of the road a number of arquebusiers, by means of which at eight o'clock in the morning they made a furious charge, in which the Lord of Vandenesse was wounded. He died of his wound shortly aftewards, regretted by the whole army. The admiral received a wound in the arm, and was obliged to be placed in a litter and taken away, leaving the whole command to Bayard, to whom he said:—

LIFE OF BAYARD.

"I pray and conjure you, for the honour and glory of the French name, to defend the artillery and the flags to-day. I consign them entirely to your fidelity, valour, and wise conduct, as there is none more capable of the task than you in the whole of the king's army, whether for bravery, experience, or counsel."

At which Bayard, much annoyed, replied that he should have wished for this honour on a more favourable and less dangerous occasion. "But," added he, "however that may be, I assure you that I will defend them so well that as long as I live they shall never come into the enemy's power."

Indeed, for two hours he made so many vigorous charges on the Spaniards, that he obliged them to rejoin the body of their army, and then he returned with his men-at-arms with as calm an air and as composed a step as if he had been walking in a garden.

The artillery and the flags were thrown forward, and in safety, when at about ten o'clock in the morning an arquebus was fired, the stone of which struck Bayard across the loins, and completely fractured his spine. When he felt the blow, his first cry was, "Jesus!" Then he added, "O God! I am slain!" Then he kissed the cross-hilt of his sword, using it as a crucifix.[1] He changed colour, and his men, seeing him stagger, went to him and wished to withdraw him from the fray. His friend D'Alègre pressed him to allow them to do so,

---

[1] The Loyal Servant adds that Bayard exclaimed: "*Miserere mei, Deus, secundum magnam misericordiam tuam.*" "Have pity on me, oh God, according to Thy great mercy." Then he waxed quite pale, as one swooning, and nearly fell, but had still strength enough to grasp the saddle-bow, and remained in this posture till a young gentleman, his steward, helped him to dismount, and placed him under a tree.

but he would not. "It is all over," he said to them. "I am a dead man, and do not wish in my last moments to turn my back to the enemy for the first time in my life." He had still strength enough left to order them to charge, seeing that the Spaniards were beginning to advance. Then he was placed by some Swiss at the foot of a tree, "so that," said he, "I may have my face towards the enemy." His steward, who was a gentleman of Dauphiny, named Jacques Jeoffre of Milieu, was bathed in tears at his side, as well as his other servants.

Bayard consoled them himself. "It is," said he, "God's will to take me to Himself. He has kept me in this world long enough, and shown me more goodness and favour than I have deserved." Then, there being no priest, he confessed to his gentleman, whom he begged to leave him where he was, because he could not be moved without feeling acute pain. The Lord d'Alègre, Provost of Paris, asked for and received his last wishes; and a Swiss captain named John Diesbac offered to remove him, for fear that he should fall into the enemy's power, but he replied to him and all the officers who surrounded him: "Let me devote the short time that remains to me to thinking of my conscience. I beg you all to leave me, for fear that you should be made prisoners; and that would be another grief for me. I am dying; you cannot relieve me in any way. All I ask of you, Lord d'Alègre, is to assure the king that I die his servant without any regret but my inability to render him further services. Give my respects to my lords the princes of France, and to all the gentlemen and captains. And now, good-bye, my good friends. I commend to you the care of my soul."

CHAPTER XXVII.

T that moment the Marquis of Pescara[1] arrived near him, and with tears in his eyes said to him: "Would to God, Lord Bayard, that I might have given all the blood I could lose without dying, to have taken you prisoner in good health! You shall know how much I have always esteemed your person, your bravery, and all the virtues that you possess, and that since I have held arms I have never known your like."

The Lord of Pescara had his own tent and bed brought immediately, had it spread close by the dying man, and himself helped him to lie upon it, kissing his hands the while. He gave him a guard, so that he should be neither crowded nor pressed upon, nor annoyed in any way, and himself brought a priest, to whom Bayard confessed with perfect consciousness and edifying piety.

---

[1] The Loyal Servant says that Pescara quoted a Spanish proverb in reference to the bravery of the knight, "The tribute of praise that my nation paid you when they said, 'Micchos Grisones, y pocos Bayardos' (many grey horses, but few Bayards, or bay ones), was not undeservedly bestowed." He adds that there were not six persons in the whole Spanish camp who did not come to see the celebrated knight.

"O generous marquis! Worthy of eternal memory. Posterity shall speak of you as long as the name of Bayard exists, and declare the bravery and virtue that rule over great hearts, even when they are in the bosoms of our enemies."

All the Spanish army hastened, both small and great, to come and admire the expiring hero. The Constable of Bourbon, who, as we have said, had passed into the emperor's service, came like the rest, and said to him:—

"Ah! Captain Bayard, how troubled I am to see you in this state. I have always loved and honoured you for the great prowess and wisdom which is in you. Ah! how much I pity you."

Bayard rallied his strength, and said to him in a steady voice:—

"My lord, I thank you; I don't pity myself. I die like an honest man. I die serving my king. You are the man to be pitied, for bearing arms against your prince, your country, and your oath."

The constable remained some time with him, and spoke of his reasons for leaving the kingdom; but Bayard exhorted him to return to the king, for that otherwise he would remain without possessions and honour all his life.

Bayard left alone, thought only of his approaching death; he recited devotedly the "miserere," after which he prayed aloud as follows:—

"My God, who hast promised a refuge in Thy mercy to the greatest sinners who return to Thee sincerely and with their whole hearts, I put all my confidence in Thee and all my hope in Thy promises. Thou art my God, my Creator, my Redeemer. I confess I have mortally offended Thee and that a thousand years' fasting on bread and water in the desert would not atone for my faults; but, my God, Thou knowest that I had resolved to be penitent if Thou hadst preserved my life. I acknowledge all my weakness—that by myself I should never have been able to merit an entrance into Thy paradise, and that no creature can obtain such joy but through Thy infinite mercy. . . . My God! my Father! forget my faults; only listen to Thine own mercy . . . . Let Thy justice be softened by the merits of the blood of Jesus Christ——"

Death interrupted his words. His first cry when he felt himself mortally wounded was the name of Jesus, and it was while invoking this adorable name that our hero gave up his soul to his Creator, on the 30th of April, 1524, aged forty-eight years.

The Spaniards showed as sincere a regret at his death as the whole of France showed. As soon as he was dead, the guard that the Marquis of Pescara had given him bore him, according to that nobleman's orders, into the nearest church, where services were said over him for two days, after which they gave the body to his gentleman and his servants, with passports, to transport it to France.

When the king heard of the death of Bayard he was sorely afflicted for many days, and paid this tribute to him: "We have lost," said he, "a great captain, whose name alone made his arms feared and honoured. Truly, he deserved more benefits and higher charges than those he had." But he felt the loss he had sustained much more acutely in the month of February following, when, after the battle of Pavia, he was taken prisoner by the emperor, and led into Spain. "If the knight Bayard," he said to the Lord of Montchenu, who followed him into his prison in Spain, "if the knight Bayard, who was valiant and experienced, had been alive and near me, my affairs no doubt would have been in better order. I should have taken and believed in his advice; I should not have separated my army, and I should not have left my entrenchment, and then his presence would have been worth a hundred captains to me, he had gained so much confidence amongst us, and so much fear from our enemies. Ah, knight Bayard! how I miss you! I should not be here if you were alive."

The body of our hero was taken to France into the province of his birth, to be placed there, according to his last wishes, near his ancestors, in the church of Creinon. The procession passed through Piedmont and Savoy; and everywhere the Duke of Savoy gave orders that it should be received with the same honours that they would have paid to a prince of the blood, that services should be performed for him in all the churches on the road, and that his body should rest there at night.

When he arrived in Dauphiny, the Court of Parliament, the Chamber of Exchequer, with the nobility and peasantry of Grenoble, went before the funeral to within half a league of the town, and conducted it into the cathedral church, where the next day they assisted at a special service, "non ducali modo sed regio apparatu," not in a ducal, but even in a kingly manner. Afterwards the body was taken not to Creinon, as he had ordered, but to half a league from the town to a convent founded by his uncle, Laurent Alleman, Bishop of Grenoble, and he was accompanied by the same procession that honoured his arrival. There he rests under a large stone at the foot of the steps of the chancel; and on the right hand side, above a door of entrance to the monastery is his bust in white marble, wearing the collar of his order, and on a white marble slab beneath there is a Latin epitaph, which the reader will find at the end of this volume.

All writers, whether while Bayard was living or since his death, French, German, Spanish, Italian, or those of other nations, have agreed, without a single exception, to praise him for all the virtues that can adorn humanity, and which were all assembled in him—piety, charity, modesty, generosity, valour, greatness of mind in danger, goodness in victory, disinterestedness, the talent of obeying and commanding; also, justice in his advice, fertility in expedients, fidelity to his king, his country, and his duty : he had all these, and his virtues cannot be better expressed than by the surname which his own age decreed to him, of the "knight without fear and without reproach."

We cannot refuse ourselves the gratification of analysing closely the eulogium which ends the supplement of the President D'Expilly.

Bayard was born with all the virtues and without any vice. He loved and feared God, always had recourse to Him in his troubles, and prayed to Him assiduously night and morning, always wishing to be alone at such times. He never refused to assist his neighbour, whether by service or money; and this he always did secretly and kindly. The poor nobles especially never had a refusal from him, whatever they asked of him. It has been reckoned that he married during his life more than a hundred poor orphan girls, gentle and simple. Widows were certain to obtain help and consolation from him. In war, he remounted one man-at-arms and gave his clothes to another, and helped to pay the debts of a third, and yet he persuaded them that it was he who owed gratitude to them. He had profitable and numerous opportunities of obtaining money by ransoms and other means; but he distributed all and kept none for himself. He never left a lodging in a conquered country without paying for what his men had taken, and when he found himself in company with certain nations whose custom it was to set fire to the places they left, he always stayed until last to preserve them from burning. He was a sworn enemy of flatterers and flattery; however great the man he was conversing with he never spoke anything but the truth to him. Slander was odious to him; he never condescended to take any part in it, but reproved it as much as it behoved him to do.

Bayard despised riches all his life, and had little esteem for the rich if they were not good also. He hated equally the hypocrite and the boaster, and punished with severity those who left their flags for the sake of plunder. To show his bravery, his wisdom in council, his prudence in action, we cannot do better than refer to what has been already written in these pages. He had passed his apprenticeship to arms under the celebrated Captain Louis d'Ars; so he all his life paid him as much respect and obedience as if he had been still his master. Finally, we must conclude our eulogium by saying that Bayard was not one of those who commenced well and slackened as they proceeded, nor of the men who terminate their career more honourably than they have commenced it. His virtues appeared in childhood; they were developed as he grew older; honours did not alter them, and they have been crowned by a glorious death and a renown that the remotest posterity will always respect.

Bayard was never actually married; but he had contracted verbally and by letter an engagement with a beautiful and noble young lady of the house of Trèque, in the Duchy of Milan, by whom he had a natural daughter, named Jane Terrail, a daughter worthy of the most virtuous of fathers.

Bayard was tall, upright, and not too stout; his face was fair, with a fresh colour, and his eyes were black and full of fire. He was extremely merry, always even-tempered, and his conversation, even on the most serious occasions, was spiced by witty remarks.

He hated the use of arquebuses, as if he had foreseen that he was doomed to die by one. "It is a shame," he would say, "that a brave man should be exposed to perish by a miserable rascal from which one cannot defend oneself." It was doubtless for this reason that he seldom gave quarter to those who fell into his hands using that weapon.

In short, if his death exactly verified the horoscope of the astrologer of Carpi, who had foretold, in 1512, that he had twelve more years to live, the rest of the prediction was not less true. "You will be rich in honour and virtue.... You will not have many of fortune's goods.... Your king will love and esteem you; but the envious will prevent his bestowing riches upon you and promoting you to the honours that you have deserved."

He was not born rich, and only increased his property by the acquisition which he made of the king's domain, an honorary right. This was a portion of the territory of Avalon that he bought for £4000 to provide his lordship of Bayard with a jurisdiction; but with this increase, all that he left at his death was not worth more than £400 annually, an admirable example of disinterestedness in a man who had been nine years lieutenant-general for the king in a large province, and who had handled immense sums of ransom money. But he often said, "What the gauntlet gains the gorget spends."

The President of Expilly says that the head of the Carthusian friars gave orders that an anniversary in perpetuity should be held throughout the whole of the order to pray for the repose of Bayard's soul; but the order must have been annulled, for it was never executed. I have seen (says M. de Berville) the rituals of the Carthusian friars in several of their houses, and no mention is made of such a command; so the writer must have been uncertain of his anecdote, or the order of the chief of the Carthusians must have been revoked.

ADDITIONAL NOTES.

Lansquenet.

LANSQUENET was a common German foot-soldier. The word is derived either from *lanze*, lance; or from *land*, land; and *knichte*, knight.

Bayard's Ancestry.

Aymond du Terrail, father of the chevalier, was noted for his great stature and strength. He received four wounds, and lost an arm, in the battle of Guignegarte, in Picardy, between Louis XI. and the Archduke of Austria, in 1479. Pierre du Terrail, grandfather of the good knight, whom he so much resembled, was renowned for his feats of arms, and was surnamed, "the sword of Terrail," *l'épée Terrail.* He was killed in battle at Montlhéry in 1465. Bayard's great-grandfather was, when aged sixty, killed at Agincourt, fighting against the English. It is evident that the Terrails were not people accustomed to die in their beds.

His great-great-grandfather, Pierre du Terrail, distinguished himself in various battles against the Flemish and English, and in 1356 fell by the side of the French King John, at the battle of Poictiers.

His great-great-great-grandfather, Robert du Terrail, after a life spent in battles, was killed in action against Anne V. de Savoie in 1337. And the father of Robert's grandfather, fighting most valiantly with his son at the battle of Tarey, was so wounded that he died in 1325.

NOTES.

Bayard's sword.

The sword of Bayard is in possession of Sir John P. Boileau, Bart. On it are two legends: "SOLI DEO GLORIA," and "VINCERE AUT MORS." Edward Cockburn Kindersley engraves the arms, but ignorantly places over them a squire's helmet. They are, Azure, a chief argent, charged with a lion issuant gules, over all a filet or bend or. A shield given by the knight to Henry VIII. at the field of the cloth of gold is in the Guards' Chamber at Windsor Castle.

Men-at-arms.

Each company consisted of 100 lancers, or men-at-arms, who were all gentlemen: hence they often refused to follow inferior infantry. A very few men-at-arms often appear to do wonders; but one must always multiply the number by six, for each lance was attended by three or four archers, an esquire, and a page, all duly armed.

Henry VIII. offered him service.

Pope Julius had made him similar proposals in 1503, offering to make him captain-general of the Church. Bayard replied that "he had but one master in heaven, which was God; and one master upon earth, which was the King of France, and that he would never serve any other." *Extract from the History of Bayard by Champier.*

Grande buffe.

"Le bon Chevalier luy vailla si grant coup sur le hault de *sa grant buffe.*" The grande buffe was a kind of bevor, the part of the armour for the head, which served to protect the lower part of the face, the visor being properly the defence of the upper; but the terms are frequently confounded. Sir Samuel Meyrick calls it the *mentonière*. Florio, in his Italian dictionary, gives buffa, the buffie, or breathing hole of a casque or headpiece. Southey confounds this with a buff-coat.

Epitaph of Bayard.

EPITAPH OF THE GOOD KNIGHT BAYARD,

IN THE CHURCH OF THE MINIMES, NEAR GRENOBLE.

Lapis hic suberbit tumulo, non titulo . . . . Ubi sepultus est heros maximus, suo ipsemet sepulchro monumentum.

D. O. M.

PETRUS TERRALIUS, Bayardus, vix puber, addictus castrensibus operis, præclarè factis tempora elusit, virtutis miraculo prælusit, primo fermè militiæ tyrocinio magnus; prodigiosæ fortitudinis, quà domi, quà foris spectacula juvenis dedit; sed illustri præsertim Italiæ theatro lauris adtexta lilia geminum in fronte honorem divisêre. Ubi virum animosa maturitas et experientia tulerunt, quæ finxit fortia facta vetustas, fecit. Bayardum Alcidi confudit impavidi et inculpati equitis cognomentum: constantis famæ vulgatu, virtutis appellationem suo nomine occupavit. Tres illum reges, lustris ferè septem, gravibus gerendi belli institutis, suæ militiæ præfectum habuerunt. Illi honorem stipendio potiorem emerito, victori triumphalia decora virtus decreverat; sed honoris currus, tot victoriis onustus, nutavit, virtutis magnitudine laboravit. Regiæ vicis, in Delphinatûs provinciâ præfecto, ingens honore fuit honore eo non egere; non concessum regni insigne, sed præmium; regem suum gladii succinctu militiæ inauguravit. Illud tandem duci semper victori deerat ut lethum vinceret: vicit: attonitæ mortis, nec ausæ luctari, feriendum se fulmineo telo objecit. Erubuit hæc, et quòd victa, et quòd immatura. Ille equo desiliens, victoriis fessus, sub arbore resedit, et vultu in hostem converso, placidè oculos et diem clausit 30 april 1524, ætatis 48.

Moriturum monumentum non morituris cineribus, N. Scipio de Polloud, D. Saint-Agnin, suis sumptibus accuravit.

THE END.

www.ingramcontent.com/pod-product-compliance
Lightning Source LLC
Chambersburg PA
CBHW031949230426
43672CB00010B/2100